Join me on a

Love Quest

Sophia Love

ISBN-13: 978-0997852776

Other books by Sophia —

The Guardian (2016)

Disclosure has begun. Meet a Guardian. Discover the dark plans & secret rituals of Humanity's Controllers (read "Illuminati"). Read here your past, present and future choices, as told by a Guardian. He came forward in 2012. He spoke for 3 years.

Find out what December 21st, 2012 really signified and what we, the human race, decided. There have been no traces of these Guardians/Executioners in our recorded history — until now.

Inclusion (2017)

A true story of contact. Countless voices. Calling from every part of creation...

"What do you want?"

Read the answers here. "*We embody a form that is more geared for flight than walking. There are wings.*"

"I am a calling member of the race you label Annunaki." "*As a group, you would label us "off planet".*

"Yet more plant-like than human-like." "*My body type is relatively humanoid. Yet that is not the point."*

"I am a representative of my species. We are a race from another star cluster inside the galaxy."

"I come from a race that is older than humanity."

sī bôrg (2017)

What does AI desire in the end? A boy - part human, part something else, answers that question in this true story.

A bird's eye view of what non-organic intelligence can look like and what it may be searching for.

All books Published by Off World Publications ©

Found at - https://www.amazon.com/Sophia-Love

(Content and cover art sole property of OWP,

Artist: https://twitter.com/doctor_dB)

Where to find more

www.sophialove.org

Here you'll find more content and every place that I am — blogs, newsletter sign ups, videos and social media accounts.

Be sure to sign up for regular updates.

Books

https://www.amazon.com/Sophia-Love

How to use this book

What you'll need

A mirror, a willing heart & about 5 minutes morning and evening.

When you'll need it

Best when done daily, yet whenever it fits in your life is perfect.

What you'll do

Take this book to the bathroom in the morning. (You'll need the mirror.)

Open to a new chapter & follow the steps in the Prelude.

Take this book to the bedroom at night.

Open to any page and read that day's notes*. Reflect.

*It may help to pick a day in the chapter you started with that morning, but it is not necessary.

Sleep with a plump heart.

What you'll feel

You are about to saturate yourself with love in its purest form.

This blows your heart wide open, leaving room for sovereignty.

You'll feel empowered.   You'll feel free.

This is fuel for bliss and bliss is where you are meant to reside.

When it ends

There is no end to the love you are capable of embodying.

How to use this book the next time

Keep it by your bedside & when so moved, open to a random page.

You'll know.

Table of Contents

Appreciation

To everyone who took that first and any subsequent Quest during the 2 years this book recalls (April 2011 to April 2013), thank you. Your sharing and love and candid stories helped all of us to discover the depths of our own hearts.

To those other numerous unnamed angels, whose participation in the process of Questing or book production or patience with either, has enabled this work to see the light of day, I appreciate all that you have so generously given.

Dedication

This book is dedicated to my deepest loves, my greatest teachers, those who know me best, my family; every single one of you, then, now and still to come.

I am so very blessed.

Sophia

5/20/2018

How, why, and what is a Love Quest

This is a Quest for love. Self-Love. It starts with you and ends with me and organically becomes us. We are One.

For the seven days these Quests last, you will be asked to look for it. The places you will look might surprise you. You may, at first, wonder if you even know what to look for. This, a result of many years and tears of misunderstanding.

This Love Quest will illustrate for you that you do, in fact, know what it looks like because you know what it *feels like*. This remembering brings instant recognition.

Love runs through you as true. There is nothing else that feels like love. It is familiar, strong and deep. You recognize it. What I have come to understand is that it is *everywhere*.

Love does not need a reason.

Each Quest will ask you to recognize it in different places and faces. You will begin to open your eyes. Eventually, you will open your heart.

You'll be asked to stretch, smile, wrap your arms around, visualize, and tiptoe into new territory. You will not have to leave your home to do this, but you will eventually want to. I promise.

You possess vast fields of unfelt possibility and oceans of promise. You will find the love that you are. You will feel your own truth. The realization of this truth is the Shift in Consciousness that we have been hearing about. The actualization of love is what we have all been waiting for.

Loving yourself is paramount.

It's seven years since the first Quest was taken. I am proof that in this one simple and sort of silly idea, results are guaranteed, but I am not the only proof. There are many of us.

You will know from where your love springs. This love will become the foundation of every posture you adopt as well as the choreographer of each stance you take. It will fuel your days and fortify your every step.

Results may differ in specifics, but not in substance. You will tentatively begin these Quests, and you will stand strong and sure-footed at the finish line. This change in your style will spring from your core. The goal of this Quest is to discover just what is held there.

Here's a bit of history, a "blast from the past" for those of you who were with us back at the start of it all, and a bit of the "inside scoop" for the newbies...

The Quests you are about to take follow an unplanned, organic sort of meandering through the struggles of my own heart. What started as an effort to forgive, grew into a full out expectation to discover joy and embody passion. This was completely unexpected at both ends, beginning and end. They lasted for two years. It was a wonderful, joyful, surprising, sometimes difficult, yet awe-inspiring 24 months.

The Love Quest is easily accomplished and fits into any schedule you have going on. It changed my life and the life of others, *thousands of others.* Join us and allow it to change yours as well.

This book gives you the essence of what was a 2-year voyage. You'll read personal references, anecdotes, reactions and historical events that accompanied and encircled our journey. Let's get started.

It was April of 2011. The first Love Quest was a Face Book event that had 4 attendees when it began. Two of them came from my family. The others were close friends. Yet it was a start.

It was called "Join me on my Love Quest". The premise was simple. Upon waking each morning, you were to look in the mirror, gaze deeply into your own eyes, and say "I forgive you". That was pretty much it.

Each day, for one week, I'd add a post and it was open for comments, thoughts, frustrations, arguments, ideas, songs, videos... whatever you were inspired to contribute.

It looked like this...

(Start below with Day #1, only pretend you are reading one # each day and then practicing or thinking about whatever it says... You get the idea.) If you'd like to begin right now, please go right ahead. Your own Quest for Love begins wherever you decide it does...

- **Day #1. Our first day of forgiveness.**

  Be sure to look in those beautiful eyes and say "I forgive you".

- **Day #2 of our Love Quest**

  Today, looking in the mirror, there came a quicker transition from ego me to the ME that exists within and beneath and around and everywhere. Looking at ME, I found recognition and happiness. I smiled then. It wasn't such a stretch to forgive myself ...

With deepest love and honor. Have an amazing journey today.

- Its day # 3.

  Interesting how forgiveness of self seems to be an act needing to be repeated... how quickly it is forgotten. The aim is complete forgiveness. Absolute and unconditional forgiveness. Repetition should give us that.

- It is the fourth day of our Love Quest.

  It is becoming a habit and developing into an EXPECTATION of forgiveness.
  Expectation is what determines the kind of life we experience.
  Noticing forgiveness is coming faster now...

- Okay, it is our fifth day of forgiveness.

  Interesting changes are happening here... forgiving all sorts of other folks...
  With much love for taking this first step...

- Love Quest Day # 6

Today there is a feeling of lightness, as if the burdens of blame have been lifted and I am free. It is intoxicating. What will happen when ALL of the chains of my own making are gone? It is a place I have not yet been, but most certainly my destination. Forgiveness will get me there.

- **We made it. It is the seventh day of forgiveness.**

So, we are here, some of us have been on this Quest for 7 days. Some for just a few, but all of us have decided to forgive ourselves completely. This is no small task and well, I find myself not wanting to stop here.

Were the seven days enough? Has the change happened and are we "done" now? Will we remain forgiven regardless of what we do in the coming days, weeks, months, years?

Should this continue? For another seven days next month, or another seven days this month, or indefinitely? Should there always be a "Love Quest" event so that others can join? (they have, you know, our numbers have grown from just 4 to now 10)

Second, what happened? What did you find?

I love you all and am so very grateful for your taking of this journey with me.

The Love Quest event is over as of today

This does not mean we stop forgiveness. Hopefully, this event was a spark that will continue for each of us a habit of love, of looking into our own eyes and seeing our truth.

We are blessed, we are divine, we are perfect. Once we accept that truth in ourselves, we will come to recognize it in everyone else as well.

It has been an honor to share this week-long journey into love with each of you. There will be another one. The effects of this week need to soak in for a moment before we do so.

Much, much love.

Reflections...

There were not too many comments for the first Love Quest, but enough. It was encouraging, and as it was a journey we were taking together, so, so powerful to have feedback. None of us were alone, this much was certain.

This book will take you through the many Love Quests that followed. It is recommended that you proceed slowly. They were written as a teaching (for us) and a learning (for myself) and it was a process that built on each preceding post, so it may help to follow them in the order that they are presented here, perhaps reading just one post each day.

Having said that, let me add that *any* day you take a moment to look at the love showing up in your life is better off for having done so. So, follow along in order, or open to random pages, either way may you be enriched and blessed and filled with the self-love that is your birth-right.

By the time this event ended on Face Book, there were over 1,000 attendees.

Before you begin your own journey, read here what some of them had to say...

"Oh, HOW BEAUTIFUL SOPHIA just like YOU thank you thank you thank you thank you for this Love Quest Journey - always invite me please " Carole S.

"Here is an eternal amount of "gratitude with an unconditional loving attitude" for everything YOU do. ROCK ON."
M.W.

"Sophia Love these were the beautiful words I woke up with this morning. Thank you." J.J.

"Dear Sophia,
Being deeply impacted by your inspirational assert on being able to become fearless... I may say becoming fearless is a daily experience, which I have attested and on my own skin, and certainly an experience which I am keen to share, when life gives me an opportunity to do so. I felt deeply happy to read your post and I have taken the liberty to translate it into Spanish to share through with friends and relatives in my Facebook page.
I wish you all the best in your journey and thank you for your

inspirational words and actions.

Kindly regards

Ricky C."

"Self-Love...comfortable, easy and effortless...sigh, I am learning,
Yes, I Am. Thank you, Sophia Love." Linda M.S.

"They are not only fun THEY are useful, it sure made me listen to
my heart, heal it and find the love of my life."   Monica L.

"Not that you need the feedback...but it can't hurt
I'm catching up on your Love Quest...
I can say I've heard it all before...and I have...in fact I've probably
said or written something very similar...and they came from both
big ME and little me at different times
But this time...THIS TIME...Sophia it rocked me to the
core...maybe it's because I'm in a different place now...maybe it's
the words YOU chose...I don't know...maybe it's not just the words
but the actual love pouring out of you as you wrote them...doesn't

even matter

I do know that the Love has been flowing from the center of my chest and enveloping everything and everyone (and I'm NOT some love and light tree hugger ;) I'm an ex-jock, sometimes rough around the edges, sometimes too intellectual, sometimes jaded, sometimes judgmental sort of guy) while, and ever since, reading your posts

Embarrassingly enough I was crying like a baby watching that young lady sing and Howie embrace her, everyone embrace her, rooting for her, identifying with her, Being her in that moment...don't tell me that people aren't inherently good...don't tell me that we don't all have immense unconditional love in our core

I'm sure that I'd have had a different reaction if I just stumbled across that vid without having first read your words...maybe not...doesn't matter."   Sean L.

"Thanks for your time, and your words are nothing less than that of a prophet in my eyes. Know that. God bless."   L. Christopher

"WE all SHINE on. All my love. U ROCK." Michael W

"Well said. Sophia an excellent composition of how it is. My own journey has brought me to this realization so many times. Only to see myself lost once again immersed once more within the illusions of the ride. Awesome. Well said my beautiful unique friend" R.E.L.

"This is one of the most beautiful and loving pieces of literature you have given to the world. I loved to read it and I love to see your writing and understanding grow more and more insightful, more and more beautiful with each word and phrase that we are so blessed to be gifted with. Thank you for sharing your love so eloquently." Zane R.B.

The Mirror

Prelude*

Officially our second Quest, this one happened later in that same month of April 2011.

The instructions are simple.

Each morning, upon awakening, look into the mirror and find your own eyes.

Once you do, say to yourself "I forgive you", followed with "I love you". Notice how you feel.

Do this *every morning for seven days in a row. This is the heart of the Love Quest.*

Welcome. Please follow along one day at a time.

This is not a race. Everyone wins on the Love Quest.

Day 1

It's your first day.

I woke up today with the words in my head - "I forgive you", "I love you".

I can feel your love; your light and it is lifting me up. I hope you are feeling mine, for it has been blasting at you all day. Bolstered with the confidence, feeling you right there with me, and me right there with you, our success is assured; we will find love.

Thank you for taking this journey with me.

Day 2

Today, when I looked at myself in the mirror, I found resolve. It was a feeling of "Yeah, you are good enough, good enough to be forgiven, good enough to love."

With that feeling I found an unexpected strength. I can be my truth, even with those who disagree, even in a whole room of disagreement.

I am enough.

Finding the love that I am, well, opens my eyes to love that is everywhere.

Look for evidence. You may be surprised.

Day 3

I have been thinking about how we learn. Your memories are associative. You only recognize what you can relate to, what you have seen before.

I am looking at myself, looking for love, offering forgiveness. Some days it is easier than other days.

Today, I forgave myself and I notice that there is less blame in my gaze.

Yesterday, I noticed less blame in my view of others. Evidence.

I am learning to forgive, and as I see myself differently, my loved ones are showing up differently too. Amazing.

We really can change our world. We just have to start with us.

I am so grateful for each of you.

Day 4

At this 'more than half way' point, I have made a startling discovery.

It is something I have known, believed, and shared, yet just a little bit ago, actually witnessed.

While speaking to someone I love dearly and know intimately, there was at first a lightness, a youthfulness, an exuberance about him. If I didn't know better, I would have said (in a sort of Hollywood way) "Did you have work done? You look younger." I didn't.

I just kept watching and listening. As he spoke, he came to a topic that caused him anxiety and AS I WATCHED, he aged.

The lines came, the darkness, the serious expression and resulting addition of YEARS.
It was fascinating. This happened twice more in the span of a ten or fifteen-minute dialogue.

I discovered, beyond doubting, that we decide with our emotions, how we look.

Yet another reason to forgive, to let it go, and to simply love.

Eternal youth and vitality is ours for the asking. Just love.

Much cheaper than cosmetic surgery, I am really inspired now.

Have an amazingly wonderful day.

Day 5

Hello.

Diligence is what comes up for me. The continuation of the journey, at this point, takes a belief that it will be worth it, a stick - to - it attitude, a conviction that YOU are worth it, that I am worth it.

You are. I am.

I have spent lots of time looking for proof of my worthiness beyond my own mirror, my own eyes — only to discover that there could be hundreds, thousands of "I love you." messages *and it would not be enough.*

The one that will sink in, comes from me.
It is the only one that matters.
Genuine love is love of self. That is the well from which all "other" love springs. Fill yourself.

You are amazing, and there is no specific attribute that makes you so. It is not your hair or your eyes or your body or your talent.

It is, simply, you.

I am honored to share this journey with you.

Day 6

You have been at this for some time now. Looking into your own eyes and saying, " I forgive you " " I love you ".

It can be tempting to just skip it now. It could be routine. There may not be too much feeling about it one way or another.

I am thinking that when that happens, you are denying its importance. You are denying YOUR importance.

Today, I laughed at myself. It was fun, playful, a little goofy as, well, I was not quite awake and looking sort of disheveled. Felt a little silly. Felt good. Glad no one was within earshot.

It is becoming ingrained, I am feeling conscious and deeply aware of my responsibility to remain so. In every moment. It is all mine. There is no one to blame. Not even, and especially not, myself.

There is no fault. You are perfect where you stand, sit, or dance. You are absolute perfection. There is no other like you and there will be no other after you. You, in your unique brilliance, are one. So, as you are, I am.

Thank you.

Day 7

You have arrived. This was a quest for love. What have you found?

I see a lighter version of me in the mirror. She smiles instantly and I recognize her, love her and enjoy her light.

I want her light to shine every day and I suspect I will continue this without an "event". *

What I notice is that the forgiveness is real. I blame less. I love more easily. Yet accepting the full, moment to moment responsibility for this life I am living, is sort of mind blowing. It goes like this - "Ok, so, I know I am divine, I know you are divine, and that you have shown up to help me discover whatever I seem to be needing to discover. But, well, ALL OF THIS IS MY CREATION?"

It seems as if I should be having a great deal more FUN.

I'm just saying. The expectation for "same old, same old" runs deeper than I understood before I took the quest. Now, well, I "get" that it is all mine. I am good with that. It is sort of like, "Now

What?"

I love you and I am so very grateful for your light.

*Blasts from the past...

This was the very beginning, and I found a query that had been included that 7th day –

> *"What is the next step? To do this again in a week, in a month? Do we do it differently? Do we do something else? I know that I am energized by the sheer number of us. We are one. It feels good."*

I also found this –

*It was from April 2011, during the birthing of these Love Quests. It was titled "**Love Quest Setbacks**" and well, it speaks for itself and maybe for you as you begin your own journey...*

"Holding on to anger is like grasping a hot coal with the intent of throwing it at someone else; you are the one who gets burned." ~ Buddha

It becomes clear when there is a slipping back, a setback, to ego self. The word "I" is heard more and more frequently from my own mouth. It may be said quietly or forcefully, either way there is no mistaking the meaning beneath it. It means that there is a return to polarity, a return to separation. No longer is it "we are one" but rather, "we are two" (or more) and let me tell you something.

YOU as in someone other than me – and that would be the first sign of ego.

The Buddha was enlightened, of that there is no doubt. Yet, by leaving his family in order to become so, he may have missed an important opportunity. A very deep love said this today –

"Isolating ourselves to feel peaceful is a misunderstanding of our relationship to each other. Better to be struggling, stumbling, learning and growing slowly together, then quickly alone. I love you too."

These words were said after a violent stumble, more like a crash. Both of us, the two entities slamming into one another, were clearly TWO, not one. It is the only way to crash you know, for if we are one than there is no other to slam into.

Our families are our best opportunities for quick enlightenment. They are gifts, propelling our growth, mirroring back every part of who we have become. We do not dress up for our families, we are not careful with what we say or how we act. We are, and they see us for what we are.

Learning to honor what they show us is perhaps the most challenging part of growth. They exist merely to show us, ourselves, and they are gifts.

Today there has been a shift and an acceptance of every member of my family, in this home and on this page, as teachers and guides and fellow light workers. In deep reverence for this journey we are on.

Evidence and Practical Oneness

Prelude

The specific instructions this month — each day for 7 days look in the mirror and smile.

Find your own eyes and rest your gaze there.

Say "I forgive you."

Say "I love you."

Say "I forgive everyone I will meet today, whether online or in person".

Welcome. Please follow along one day at a time.

This is not a race. Everyone wins on the Love Quest.

Day 1

Today, the sun is shining, I heard the birds very, very early and it was as if they were saying "Wake Up. Today is the day."

And so I did. I woke up with a smile, looked at myself and loved myself, forgave myself and declared, out loud, that I loved and forgave everyone else I would meet today.

The universe, just about instantly, showed me some versions of myself that said "No, you don't love me, or forgive me. Are you kidding me? Get over yourself."

So, I ignored those versions of myself, as I knew they were not ME. I remembered that I was the one here in this physical body, and I had all the power. I loved anyway. It was a glorious morning, once I remembered it was. *

I am nervous, excited and hopeful. This can work. This has to work. This is the reason we are here. We are here to love.

Thank you for your love.

In Lak'ech. *(A Mayan phrase meaning: You are my other self. We are one.)*

Day 2

It is the second day. Here are some thoughts I am having*...

This Quest is about forgiveness, yet inside I am feeling conflicted about my own reaction to recent events and the humans involved in them.

Today's post will end here. It is a day of contemplation for me.

Thank you for sharing this journey.

Day 3

Hello.

In our town, on the first Tuesday of each month, there is a siren check and I just heard it. It reminds me that sometimes we need something extra ordinary to GET OUR ATTENTION.

Perhaps we have been asleep. Perhaps we have been thinking everything is ok. These alarms, sirens, etc... tell us, no, there is something you must do. You have missed this, pay attention.

We do that for each other. Maybe not so obviously as a siren, but in our relationships, we get reminders. Reminders that tell us our ego is still operating here... we are not coming from love... not in this case, in this relationship.

We are angels for each other. Those that have come to help us to get this, *this time*, are perhaps not those we find it easy to be with. They may be the ones that drive us nuts. They are our deepest loves. Our angels. They have volunteered to show up a certain way so that we would get it, whatever it may be. They are a challenge. As we are for them.

Today I stand in appreciation for my angel, my mate, my beloved. He shows me the worst of myself and the best of myself. In this quest for forgiveness of me, I find that he is right there, giving me immediate opportunities to forgive HIM.

He is my own personal siren. Just when I think "I've got this. I think I have figured this out." He sort of taps me on the shoulder and does something that brings out my most unforgiving self.

It is to him primarily, and to every other of my angels, who have shown up at various times in my life, that I say "I am so sorry. Please forgive me. I love you. Thank you. I release you."

Thank you for sharing this journey with me.

Day 4

Hello.

How are you doing? We are on the down side of the week-long quest; we have come half way.

I am discovering a deep understanding of the importance of forgiveness. It is not a small thing. It stands at the core of our ideas of separation.

If I am able to maintain ANY idea of anger at an action brought on by you, then I am seeing you as separate from me. So separate, in fact, that I feel justified in judging you.

This is at the root of polarity. This is the idea that begets war. This is what we are all attempting to let go of, in order to achieve the state of oneness which defines enlightenment.

It starts with me. If I can look in my own eyes and understand and love her, regardless of who she has ever shown up as, then I will understand unconditional love.

There is so much here to talk about... we have all misunderstood.

We are now trying to understand. It is not about you - vs - me. It is about us.

This is much easier to do INTELLECTUALLY, than physically; in real time, off of Face Book, Twitter and Instagram; in our kitchens, in our living rooms, and in our bedrooms. This is why there is a Love Quest. It is personal and we are all individually on the same path.

Thank you.

Day 5

So today feels different.

There was a visible shifting last night, that seemed to be building for days. A settling in, as if momentum had been building, more and more pieces were being properly placed and last night, a really important piece found its way and arrived.

It was an "ahhh" moment, a sigh of relief was silently breathed, and then there was a relaxing, snuggling down and getting comfortable.

Letting go is, I think, more of a gift for myself perhaps than it is for the person I am forgiving. Yes, and since we are one, well, the benefits are exponential.

Thank you for sharing this journey with all of us. Regardless of where you are today, we are together, and I love you.

Day 6

Hello there.

Today there is a deep knowing of oneness. I feel an appreciation for everyone I see...each eye and skin and hair color are my own, each attribute one I share, each skill one I too have perfected as well as each stumble I have taken. All mine, all yours, all ours.

Unity is not something I can intellectualize any longer. I feel it now. It is me, I am you, they are us, we are one. Such peace in that, such wonder, such love.

I am already thinking of our next quest. Not to worry, it will be next month as there must be time for this to "cook"; I believe, now, that it will revolve around the things we are saying to ourselves when we are NOT looking in our mirrors and saying "I forgive you and I love you".

For it is those things, those repetitive thoughts, habitual feelings of "I'm not good enough" in some way or another, that cause us to trip on this quest for love.

They are like addictions, and to stop them will take herculean effort, yet they are stoppable - for together, we can do whatever we set our hearts to do.

I love you. I am better because you are in my life. Thank you.

Day 7

Hello.

Today we look at ourselves once more and say "I forgive you and I love you." Each time we say it, it reaches the ears of all of us.

We are one. As I let myself off the hook, I released you as well. Free, I was able to look around and see what else there was to notice.

I noticed love. I noticed compassion. I noticed YOU.

This journey we are on and have been on, not just this week but this LIFE, is filled with each other.

We are the stuff of God, stardust, the force for creation.... the beauty we hold is beyond description, the love we are immense.

That is why we came together...to enjoy each other; to laugh with, swim with, shout with, speak to, whisper to, dance with, run with, cry with, look at, smell and taste ~ each other.

It is about us. We are the miracles. The ones we are waiting for.

You and I, him and her, they, them, us.

Letting go of the stories in our heads, the ones that keep us busy and NOT NOTICING each other, begins with forgiveness. This leads to love.

Our quest will continue in a few weeks. I am so profoundly fortunate
to share this journey with each of you, with all of you. Thank you.

You are a gift.

*Blasts from the past...

This Quest was happening in May of 2011. So were lots of other things, both globally and locally. Here are a few notes from that time.

From Day 1

It is an interesting thing that today (our first day) is Global Love Day and Good Karma Day...seems like the universe is also cooperating... she wants to be sure we all get this love thing...

From Day 2

With the killing of Osama Bin Laden, I have seen many, many reactions. I am not sure what the "right" reaction is, as there is no "right" or "wrong", yet inside I am feeling that well, forgiveness of all is forgiveness of all.

I was devastated personally by the Sept. 11th events, as we all were. Yet to shoot fireworks and set up a Facebook page to "like", celebrating a killing, well, for me that does not resonate.

We are one.

I am saddened. This cannot be a partial shift, we cannot believe that some of us are wrong and deserve judgment. This love quest exists because of this kind of thinking, inside of me, perhaps inside of you as well. I love you.

From Day 5

This idea of forgiveness seems to be going viral. I must have seen half a dozen video links on forgiveness just yesterday. This, as opposed to never seeing them. I like this reality my new awareness is creating. Rather than seeing a constant stream of videos about what is wrong with our world, I am seeing what is good. I am feeling the support of many who are on the same page.

Addictions

Prelude

The specific instructions this month — each day for 7 days look in the mirror and smile.

Find your own eyes and rest your gaze there.

Say "I forgive you."   Say "I love you."

Throughout your day, you will notice thoughts that are repetitive and unproductive, unforgiving and unloving; they are negative. They are yours and they need not be rejected. Notice them. Love them. Hug them. Release them.

Visualize yourself as you are thinking them and gently explain that you aren't doing that any longer. You are loving yourself and learning to love your life. It's all okay and you are fine.

This is loving tenderness. Give it to yourself for 7 days in a row. It won't take long. No one will even know you are doing it, no one but you that is.

This is the heart of this Love Quest.

Welcome. Please follow along one day at a time.

This is not a race. Everyone wins on the Love Quest.

Day 1

Today I woke up with a head full of thoughts to love, hug and release. These thoughts have been my *always* addictions and they do not serve me. They built a me that was filled with anger and sadness.

This is not who I am. Yet, it is who I have been. I cannot deny all parts of me that I don't think are attractive. In order to love myself, I must love ALL of myself. If I am looking for acceptance, I must accept everything, the ugly, the angry, the frustrated, the crabby, the sad.

So, for this first day I am well armed.

I have plenty to accept, plenty to love.

These repetitive thoughts are addictions. No less powerful than heroin, for they can ruin a life. They can become the point of a life. They are the need you have/I have that must be supplied. They set me up for the specific chemical cocktail my brain wants. They are relentless, persistent, and cunning.

Take "sad", a favorite of mine. There are stories in the news that give me the feeling. There is the scale (if I am dieting). There are my children, if they "disappoint" me with their behavior. There is my lover, my friend... the list goes on and on.

Once I see that I have, yet again, felt sadness over something, what I need to do is recognize it. Realize that it is always my choice. See myself happy, strong, smiling, pleased and hug the version of me that is sad. See ME (happy ME) tell me (sad me) that *"I love you, but you will have to take a back seat over here. I am doing "happy" now."*

It is not a denial of the feeling or thought, it is a refusal to use it as a drug.

Thank you for your willingness to take this journey with me.

I love you.

Day 2

Hello.

It is our second day and mine has been filled with activity. On days like this I find myself on automatic pilot...running, often without a lot of thought.

As I was driving a lot, I was considering something I have noticed about this Quest. It is work. This is not the hearts and diamonds kind of love, this is tough love.

I have had to stop myself many times, and visualize, visualize, visualize. I see this me, the one telling me what it has always been telling me, to be most un-becoming. It is difficult to love her completely.

Right now, she is sitting on the front steps of my childhood home. She does not look very happy.

As I approach her, and go to hug her, she is not really receptive. She is deep in her discomfort, in her belief about herself as "less than". This is not a vision I enjoy.

Yet it is a me I know intimately. It is me, the one I have built on a foundation of lies. It is the me that accepts a lesser version of me, of my life, of my abilities.

It is most definitely not ME. The ME that is now hugging her, is powerful and strong. She is sure footed and sure of herself. She loves and understands, sees and accepts, then explains, gently: "I love you. But that is not who I am now."

There is so much love in a healthy denial of self-abuse.

Addictions are abusive. They eat at you with fear and with un-truths. They are weak when confronted with love.

Make no mistake, they are no match for you.

You are beautiful and strong and powerful and incredible and just right. You are a piece of God, and as one of my favorite angels used to say, *"God doesn't make junk."*

Remember to love ALL OF YOU. You are not wrong, or bad, or stupid or ugly, or old, or fat, or sick, or weak, or poor or out of luck. You have been mistaken. Tell yourself the truth now, tell it to yourself again and again and again.

You are love. You are magnificent. You are all that and even more. Thank you for sharing this moment with me.

Day 3

Hello and thank you for showing up.

It is a beautiful day and filled with promise for more to come.

We are the brave, the beautiful, the magnificent. We are the ones we are waiting for.

With love, self-love, we are transforming ourselves into powerful beings of love and light, strength and compassion. There will be, *there IS*, nothing we cannot comprehend and move through with love.

Love is the most powerful force in the universe. It is not money or hate or military might. It is love. We have that, in abundance. It does not cost anything.

It is here, within, yours for the taking.

Love. Self-love. It starts with awareness of who you are. It starts by listening to that voice within.

It is not hating that voice when it doubts your magnificence. It is tenderly and definitively telling it to stand down. This is not who you are. You are love and you know that now.

Love is not divisive and so there can be no parts of you to hate. It does not work that way. You cannot be a light worker, a being of peace, a care-giver, and hate your boss or your government or your waistline or your ex-wife. If you are love, then so are they, *so are all parts of you*. Every one of us, every part of us.

We are so covered in layers of hate to be almost hidden.

Not anymore. Your light is shining from my computer screen. I see it in your words, your pictures, your "likes", your xox's... I feel it.

Keep loving. It is so, so powerful. Thank you for loving me, for taking the quest, for being here.

Day 4

Hey there.

Thank you for being here. I feel, I hope you all feel, NOT ALONE. We aren't, you know. We are really all in this together, cheering each other on and leading the way and following along.

In reality, this is a dream. Quantum physics tells us this. Matter is mostly air, empty space. I don't have anything negative that is keeping me from loving myself. Not really. I just love myself. I just love you. In reality that is.

On this place called earth, we have anger and illness and expectation and disappointment and loss. It is just pretend. It is set up this way. WE set it up that way.

If you never lose anything, you may not understand its value. If you are not weak, you may not appreciate what it is to be vital. If you are not lonely, you may not understand what it means to finally find someone to fill that emptiness. It is an illusion. We are master magicians. We set up this game ourselves. To figure it out. To get, to really "grock", love.

In truth love is what we are. Children know this. They have easy smiles and sparkling eyes and they engage every other soul they run into on their journey. Until grownups begin to explain to them the concept of danger.

We warn others because we ourselves are afraid. It is time to stop being afraid. It is time to start loving. Love cannot truly exist where there is fear.

It takes courage to look at ourselves. Look at what we have considered ugly, or weak, or just not good. Look at that voice telling us how wrong we are and tell it *"No, I don't do that anymore. You have had your turn. IT'S MY TURN NOW."*

We can do so with love. We can do so tenderly. We can look at our fears and our self-hatred and we can love them BECAUSE WE KNOW THE SECRET. THEY ARE NOT TRUTH.

The truth is that we are love. You are eternal beings of love. Regardless of what you have ever "done", who you have ever "been" on this earth, you are forgiven. You are perfection. You are love. You came now, to love now, to be whole now, to realize NOW the perfection of you so that others, seeing your light, would then realize their own perfection.

It is in this way that the planet will raise its vibration. It starts with each of you. We are one.

Day 5

I will keep it short today, yesterday was akin to
"War and Peace".

I love you. You are doing a fine job.

Remember that YOU are the one you have been waiting for. It is
not up to your parents or lovers or children or friends to love you
into feeling good. It is up to you. You must accept and
acknowledge your perfection and love yourself up. For you. For us.
For the planet.

Just love and you will find your cup always full.

Today I see who I am, completely, and I accept her as divinity. I
love her. She was built with all the knowledge I had at the time,
and she is worthy of love. She is worthy of MY love. She is
perfection. As are you.

It starts and ends with us. I love you.

Day 6

It is all about choice.

It comes to this. We can choose to feel frustration or choose to love. We can choose to feel sad or choose to love. We can choose angry or choose love. We can choose to hate our bodies or choose to love all parts of ourselves.

It is us that makes the final choice. It is not your boss or your mirror or the scale or your mate or your government. It is you.

Loving you - while seeing who you are and where you are and who you are with; is the only option. *It is not that you can hate yourself into improvement.*

It is that you must love yourself. Then, from a point of love, you lovingly decide to change something that no longer serves you, if that is what you choose.

This thing, the thing you lovingly wish to change, does not diminish you or your love or your light. It is just that, from your current perspective, it no longer serves the vision of yourself you hold now.

That's it. There is no right "you" or wrong "you". There is just you. Perfect, light filled, love filled, glorious you. These shells and these illusory trappings neither diminish nor enhance the beauty of an eternal one such as you. The suit you are wearing and the set on which you are acting was chosen, by YOU.

It may be time to choose another set or alter the shell, but that is just a change of scene or costume or fellow actors, not a change of you. YOU ARE PERFECT. No need to alter that.

I love you.

Day 7

It has been an interesting week. I have come to understand some things at a deeper level. In looking within, I have discovered judgment.

I am so very grateful for you, for your willingness to go here with me. For me, this was a vast area of undiscovered truth. They say the ocean is mostly unexplored, well, so am I.

This week I looked at me and judged. Then, in no small part due to this quest and to you, I re-assessed my judgment. How can it be that I do not love?

I found some truth, and I suspect, with time and further quests, I will find some more. I found that love has no room for judgment. That love does not co-exist with fear. I found that my concept of perfection is based on a dream and that in truth, perfection is what I am.

How can it be that you, that I, am anything less than perfect?

You are a piece of divinity. It is perhaps "sin", in the truest sense, to believe in failure.

There is no failure. This is all as planned. You, me, your body, my body, your job, my job, your life, my life, your planet, my planet. We made this, so that we would learn, beyond doubt, what it means to love. What it means to hold the "keys to the kingdom" and create consciously, purely and absolutely with intention.

It starts with you. Love the you that sits here, reading this note. Love her/him completely for she/he was lovingly created so that you'd come to master this dream.

You are a gift. Treasure yourself truly and from that point of appreciation you will come to know agape.

I love you.

Blame

Prelude

As the Quests continue, we begin to look at aspects, things that stop us from self-love.

These things have become addictions, and they are evident in our "ego", which speaks to us with volume and clarity. It is unmistakable once identified. This Quest will look squarely at the emotions that feed our ego. We will learn how to identify them (the emotions that we seem to repeat again, and again) and it (our ego, personality self).

Instructions for this Quest

Each morning for 7 days, look in the mirror and greet yourself with a smile and "I see you." "I know you." "I am in charge today." "I choose happy."

This Quest considers responsibility. Each time something shows up that tempts you to blame another, to experience feelings that are all too familiar as well as unpleasant — stop and remember who is in charge of your life and of your happiness. It is you.

Welcome. Please follow along one day at a time.

This is not a race. Everyone wins on the Love Quest.

Day 1

On this first day I notice pockets of blame and anger. Inside these pockets is this little version of me, feeling powerless to change a situation, and feeling sad because of that. It is not true.

You are never powerless. You have merely blurred your vision and need to re-focus your lens. It is pointed in the wrong direction. When you see where to focus it, you will see clearly.

It is always on you. There is no other. This is an illusion. Any residual anger or excuse for non-gratification of any kind will always come back to you. Every time.

Your ego self is fully aware of the most vital feelings for you and will use them every time. It is here you must utilize what you know about love. It always returns to source, to you.

It is up to you to feel differently now. Decide what you want to feel and then feel that. Your world will reflect back for you whatever decision you make.

This is a dream. It is dictated by your emotions. Your emotions feed your addictions. Your ego is the voice of your addictions.

Your approach to life from your ego-self will be to create scenario's that feed the addictions you have.

Addictions can be loved and absorbed and changed into something that serves you. The trick is to love them first, realize from where they spring, and then let them go.

I am working on happy. It will become my point of power.

I love you. Thank you for joining this quest with me.

Day 2

Hello.

On this second day* I have a true story. It has had a powerful effect on me and my loved ones, and I am hoping it will for you as well.

Yesterday, it was beautiful here, and once evening came, I found myself relaxing on the couch with my Beloved. We were watching a video online. We were aware that it was beginning to rain.

Our son was at a friend's house in our town. I got a text message from him asking if we were okay. I replied. "Yes, why?". He asked, "You have power?" I said "We do". We kept watching the video.

An hour or so later, he returned with tales of transformers blowing up, red and green lightening, and power outages ALL OVER TOWN. He said "There are trees blown down everywhere, it's pitch black, UNTIL YOU GET HERE. THERE IS NO POWER ANYWHERE NEAR HERE. HOUSES ON THIS STREET ARE OUT. EXCEPT RIGHT HERE."

We had no idea. We were blissfully engaged in each other and the movie we were watching. The storm had no reality for us *and so it did not affect us.* There are logical reasons perhaps for this, but within a few feet of us 280,000 homes are today without power. We are not. I believe that the reason we are not, is because the storm was not part of our reality last night.

We create every part of our lives. Once we accept this idea, it becomes the next logical step to take that we are creating EVERY MOMENT THAT IS WITHIN EVERY PART OF OUR LIVES.

It is our awareness of what is real that makes it so.

Do you understand what I am saying? *We were not aware of the storm, that apparently raged all around us, and so it did not affect us.* We did not stop the storm, that is not what I am saying. Yet, while we were in the same "dream" and physical location as this very active storm, we were not hindered by it.

This is a dream you are having. Your awareness of things makes them a part of your life. **The next dimension may very well be nothing more than a change of focus.** It is why those in power spend so much money to get us to be afraid of the enemy or the next epidemic. If we focus on fear, we are powerless.

This quest is about realizing your power. It is what makes us so powerful, and why so many work so hard to diminish our awareness of it. Focus only on what you want to be real for you, and it becomes so.

Here, in my home, we are blown away by what happened last night. *It was like WE WERE LIVING IN ANOTHER REALITY.*

I believe, when all is said and done, that this "jump to the next dimension" or "shift in consciousness", is nothing more than a change of focus. Focus on you. You are love. You are the most powerful force in the universe. It is at your command once you truly "get" that it is yours.

Just love. Start with you. Listen to your heart and it becomes encouraged. It then speaks louder and louder, so loud that raging storms cannot drown it out.

I love you. Thank you for hearing my story.

Day 3

Hello there.

This quest is about feeling your own power. You understand that in order to feel empowered you have to give up the whole notion of blame. Empowerment is a choice.

How you feel is your choice. You have no power, not really, over your children or your parents or your lovers or your employer's actions. Your power rests in how you feel.

You can choose anger or sadness, but in truth, this will have no effect on anyone but you. The "other" will do what they will do, regardless of what you feel about it.

We have all heard about the "Law of Attraction". *In choosing to be happy, regardless of what is going on around you, you will, over time, be sustained by a frequency that allows only things within that happy 'vibe'.* It is true. Your choices each moment have a residual effect. You effect the quantum field and eventually, through repetition, you will experience what your underlying intent is.

Here is another story (a shorter one). To drive anyplace from my home, you have to pull out onto a very busy street. You may wait more than five full minutes for a free spot in which to pull out. I decided a few years back that I would have NO TRAFFIC at that corner; that whenever I got to that corner, I'd immediately be able to pull out.

It took a while, and I had to be persistent, but today there are NEVER CARS when I get to that corner. We used to laugh about it, because when my partner used my car, he didn't have any traffic either, and we decided it was because I had affected the field in my car. In his own car, when he was driving, the traffic persisted.

When my car got there, my intent took over, regardless of whether or not I was driving. We laughed about that.

It is about choice. This is a dream. You are at the wheel of every moment. It really is about whatever you decide is real.

What happens, I think, is that when results are not immediate, we give up and "blame" it on society, or genetics, or luck or whatever. It takes persistence, belief and trust. You have *to know* that it's only you. The universe has no choice but to reflect back to you whatever you expect; traffic, storms, illness, health, wealth, poverty, happiness, love. It is all yours by choice. Your choice.

Choose what serves you. Every time. Eventually, your world will catch up, once the remnants of all those previous choices get played out. The power has always been yours, believe that.

I love you. Thank you.

Day 4

Hello there.

I hope this finds you aware and thinking. There are so many different aspects of love to consider.

In this life, we are bombarded with rules and habits and sensations and memories; all of which contribute to our interpretation of who we are, of who we "should" be.

The only one who knows who you "should" be, is you. You have grown up watching and listening and learning and practicing to "be". It may have been that you wanted to be a fireman, a doctor, a preacher, a teacher, a mother, a father or a dancer. These are roles and yes, they require practice and learning. They define what you do, not who you are.

You are not practicing now. You are. There is nothing else to know.

Love is the very core of your being. That part of you speaks in every quiet moment of truth you have. It whispers "yes" when you are genuinely happy. It shouts "yes" when your light fills the room. You know these moments.

You may have relegated them to weekends, or just to random fun moments, but you know them when they arrive. They are love, expressed and felt, seen and shared, appreciated and enjoyed. They are who YOU are. You are love.

When you are at your happiest, you are following your divinity, your heart, your soul, your truth, your path. It is as simple as that. Listen to the joy in your heart and from your soul. It is telling you truth.

No one knows your truth but you. Trust. Love. Be.

You are meant to be magnificent. It is why you came.

You came to show us how it is done.

Thank you for showing me the way.

With deepest gratitude, I love you.

Day 5

Hi. How has today been so far?

You have begun to understand that your life has been directed by choices you've made, and no other.

It is easy, once you do, to fall into blame and fault finding and numerous reasons to hate yourself. Don't.

See who you are, who you have been, and embrace her/him. Tenderly. We could all use a little tenderness. Some love. Hug yourself. Your imagination is the most powerful tool you have.

Your imagination is what has created your life. If you imagine yourself loved, you feel loved and you exude love and you see love and you have love. If you imagine yourself sad, you feel sad and you exude sadness and you see sad movies, people, news, situations and you have sadness.

Decide what you have and who you are and imagine yourself THERE.

Eventually, your life will comply. It has no choice. You are the master of your universe. It is not me, or your mother or your diagnosis or your luck. It is you.

It takes persistence and belief but you are up to this. You chose this. You volunteered to be here; to choose and to choose again.

Your light shines for all of us to learn from and grow by and share with. The combination of our light together illuminates this moment now. It is brilliant.

Thank you for showing up.

Day 6

Hello there.

I have been thinking about conscious choice. It is one thing to understand that your life is your choice. It is another thing to deliberately choose your life.

You must first be aware that choice is an option. With awareness can come a huge sense of overwhelm. As in, "This is all MY fault?".

Then blame and fault finding can emerge. Cut it out. It does not serve you. It only holds you in a negative vibratory pattern, creating more of what you don't want.

Love yourself. Accept that each choice made was done so with all of the information you had at the moment.

It is a new moment. You have more information. Time to make a new choice. You may want to re-route.

It can take a while. There may be many "oops" moments, where, habit and unconscious response kicked in. You may say or do something you have always done, that has led you down the path you are now trying to alter.

It is ok. Love yourself and notice. Next time the new response will come quicker, you will say a new thing, do a new thing. Take note when this happens. Smile.

Up until today, it has been about changing habitual thoughts and ways of being in the world.

Now it is time to CREATE NEW WAYS of being in the world. It is from a point of power that you will become the enlightened soul you are meant to be now. Decide who you are.

You are not here to merely react to your world as it revolves around you. You are here to ACT. *This is your world.*

Who are you? What does a person like that say? What does a person in that position look like? What does a person like that do? Where does a person like that go?

It is time to make your life the one you are dreaming of.
You have the power.
Just follow your heart.

It is an honor to share your journey. Thank you.

Day 7

Today we have completed our Quest.

We began with a goal. Our goal was to discover and accept responsibility for these lives we lead. We have done so.

This quest goes on now, regardless of the calendar. It does. It always will. That is how it works with creation.

You dream, you create, you attain, you celebrate (or you reflect). Then, you dream again.

Isn't it wonderful? There is no end, until and unless we decide to end it. We choose our life. This is a life of self-determination.

We have chosen to come here and live in a world that presents us continuously with polarity and reasons to judge... and while being here, immersed in all of these opposing viewpoints...to decide our life, to choose our life, to live our life.

Who will we be? Where will we live? What will we do? What does it mean?

It is not a question of who you are. You are LOVE. You are

LIGHT.

It is only the rest of it you choose. All of it you can change your mind about and choose again.

You are wearing a 3-Dimensional suit that walks around with opinions and an ego that is working very hard to keep you here, focused on whatever currently has you spinning.

It merely takes a change of focus to alter your life. A change of YOUR focus. Not your parents or your boss or your government or your spouse. You. You have the controls.

Spin about something that serves you. Love serves you. It is who you are. How you express that love is determined by your unique self. No one else has your eyes or viewpoint or skills or preference. Not exactly.

You are perfect where you stand and came here, to this earth, right now, to perfectly express your remarkable self. We are so blessed to watch you do so. Thank you.

You are appreciated more than you know.

*Blasts from the past

At this point, the Quests became more organic. In our sharing we would notice things and then those things became part of subsequent Quests. This Quest combined creation with blame and responsibility.

From Day 2

This Quest began on the day of the Summer Solstice, which was June 21st, 2011. This story happened on that day. This was real physical evidence of our power to create. ¼ of a million homes lost their power that night, including our neighbors on all sides, while we did not.

Noticing

Prelude

> This Quest asks you to notice what love is. You are surrounded by your every day and most likely missing it, perhaps not really aware of what to look for.
>
> Each day for 7 days, upon waking, look into the mirror and meet yourself there.
>
> Look into your own eyes.
>
> Say "Hello. I love you".
>
> Wait for that to sink in.
>
> Now look deeper and say "I will not take you for granted today."
>
> Wait for that to settle in and then say "I will allow today to surprise me, to show me love."

Welcome. Please follow along one day at a time.

This is not a race. Everyone wins on the Love Quest.

Day 1

Hello. On this first day, I find myself wondering about this compulsion to Dissatisfaction. It is not so much walking around angry or even annoyed all the time. It is just a general "ho-hum" attitude to most things.

If I were to simply pay attention, life would astound me. I am surrounded by light. It emanates from those I live with, from the trees and flowers, from my cat. As I write this I am receiving confirmation that this is the right track...sparks shoot through my fingers to the keyboard. Very cool*.

We chose this. We are here with purpose. Individual steps are not identical yet overall mission is. We have come to awaken, not only ourselves but each other. We are connected at our core. We are one. Love resonates with each of us because Love is ALL of us. You are an individual expression of the ONE. You and I are the same.

You have come to spread your light. Frustration and anger covers that which you are, and it is difficult for me to make out your essence.

This morning my son overslept. He awoke and began to shout at me to "get going" because of his lateness (I was driving him). Not too long ago I would have yelled back. Something about it not being my fault, etc.

Today I noticed (perhaps because of our Quest) that he is yelling at himself, and I have nothing to do with it. I did not react with words. I felt my body tense and heat course through me. Then I said nothing and noticed it pass. It did. There was no further yelling. The moment moved on.

Now this may not sound like much, yet I noticed that the bright light that is my son was clouded with worry this morning. He is very young and yet has taken on worry as a sign of "growing up". Most likely I gave that to him, as my mother did to me.

Worry is not something that we need. Neither concern, nor annoyance or frustration. Every moment we have planned, and it is ours to savor. It will inevitably move on to the next moment. We need only watch it.

Love is available in each moment. Look at your life with the idea that it is only love. You put it there. You can do with it whatever you wish. You can appreciate it, notice it or fight it. Either way will not change its essence, it will unfold and move on regardless.

Today I will pay attention to the everyday things and people I have taken for granted and allow them to astound me. Thank you for taking this journey with me. I love you.

Day 2

Hello again.

I have been thinking about this Quest, as well as the others we've taken...

It is all about choice. There is a truth that reaches ever deeper with each new realization. It surrounds the statement "You are the creator of your life". Most of us on this journey to awakening and awareness will agree with that. It is one thing to agree intellectually with a truth, and another thing altogether to KNOW a truth.

You have to LIVE there, and while there, notice what is happening. The idea of watching your anger or frustration pass without reacting makes sense in an obvious way. You will feel better. The negative reaction will not escalate. The "other" who seems to be causing your reaction will have nothing to further extend the moment with. Peace will ensue. You will feel better. You may even smile.

There is more than just this moment. Notice that our intentions have a cumulative effect. It gets easier and easier with repetition. There will be more things to upset you, certainly, yet with each refusal to react, your love grows ever stronger.

This is how we create our life. It is birthed in each small moment. As your love grows, others will notice. They will feel better too. You will feel their love grow. The focus of your life will be about ease and comfort and peace and collaboration. Gradually, seamlessly, you will notice that a shift has occurred.

This, I believe, is the shift in consciousness, also known as the shift of the ages, also referred to as Ascension. There is a deeper and deeper line that separates unity consciousness from polarity consciousness. It just becomes crystal clear.

You cannot love everyone on one "side", while cursing at all those on the other "side" and consider yourself to be expressing solidarity or unity. That is not an expression of oneness. It is all about choice. Either you express love or you don't. There are no "sides" to a circle.

As you choose peace in each moment, you change your life and those with whom you live. As they choose peace, it ripples out further and further. There are no small moments. There is no insignificant act of love.

We are the change we are looking for. We are changing, shifting, together, as one. The magic is us.

Day 3

It is a gift to be able to speak to you each day. You help to ground me in truth. Thank you.

We are each searching for the same thing. We are searching for love. The truth is that WE ARE LOVE. The love that we are is the inner lining of this human suit we are each wearing.

You have forgotten. It is time to remember. This quest for love is centered on watching anger and sadness pass, without becoming angry and sad. There is a reason you can do that, and with practice it will get easier. Here is the secret.

The more you love yourself, the less "others" will have any effect on you. **The strength of you resides in your unconditional self-love.**

The power of you exists for all to see, once you stand, unmovable in the conviction that YOU ARE LOVE.

You are love. Once you own this truth, it will not matter what arises in your life. You will, from a new vantage point, watch it pass. You will know it has no real power over you. It is not you and it is not a problem. It is life and as change is inevitable, it will change.

Others will love you or not, and it will not change you. Their love will not define who you are. You are love, all by yourself. You are perfection. You are priceless. You are divine.

There is no condition that changes the truth of you. You have taken on this form, at this time, to experience this life. There will be other forms and other lives. This life now, is where you are focused. Why not enjoy it?

You came here to create, knowing the field was full of opposition. White is ever so much more radiant against black.

Love the one that is you, that is us. You are brilliant particles of one glorious life - which is us. It is time to stand in your power and shine.

Day 4

We are midpoint on this particular journey.

How are you doing? We are half way there, yet just where are we going? And what does half way really mean anyway? Time is an illusory construct. It exists as it does only in this dimension, for us on earth.

So, let's just say we are on our way. The places we are headed are individually determined. We are choosing them now, and now and now. We have all chosen to be here, together, now, searching for that which we are. What we are searching for is love.

It sounds paradoxical. How can you find what you already are? Where do you look?

It is not a looking so much, as a feeling. You will know the Quest was successful when you feel loved. When you can think about you and smile. When you are not hating your body or your last decision. When that feel good moment is just inside you all the time.

This moment is akin to the feeling you get when holding a baby, making love, looking in the eyes of a loved one or gazing at our beautiful Mother Earth. This is a reflection of truth, the truth of you. You are this moment in its very essence. It is how you were meant to feel, all the time.

This is the reason to allow anger or sadness to pass when it arises. If you allow it to continue, you are the one who suffers. It is not the "other". It is you.

Without the suffering of sadness or anger or blame, you will feel the love that you are. Once you understand that love, you will be that love. In whatever places you find yourself, you will give that love away and those that receive it will do the same, and on and on and on.... Oneness.

Thank you. You are changing the world from your laptop, creating unity with a keystroke. You are indeed a powerful creator. It is an honor to witness.

Day 5*

It is a perfect idea to look for love. Entire industries are built on that very premise. They spring from the thought that love is something found outside of ourselves, that it is only found in the "other", in our one true love. This makes a great Hollywood film, but it is not entirely true.

The truth is that love exists as you. You see it reflected in others, because they mirror the love that you are. You see it reflected in Mother Earth, because she too, mirrors back who you are. You are love.

The hardest person to love unconditionally, is YOU. You are the one you know best. Your promise, your "failings", all are intimate companions in your heart. It is time to realize that each component of you, each part, each fault, each skill, each win, each loss, is a piece of perfection.

There is an ability to purchase perfection in a store. If you want a flower without brown spots, that needs no water or sunlight or special location, you can buy plastic or silk ones. Factories turn out hundreds, maybe thousands of them, all the same, all perfect. But beautiful? There is a certain symmetry to a shelf full of fake flowers, and some would call that beautiful.

Imagine the contrast of that shelf to an entire field of wildflowers, with the scent and the sun and the weeds and the trees and the LIFE. You are one of those wildflowers, and you are living in a field, surrounded by the whole.

Each flower is unique and free, adding its brilliance to the whole. Love is like that. It looks different because it is incomprehensibly beautiful, and its beauty lies in its imperfections.

I am an imperfect flower, as are you, as is everyone else in this field called humanity, and we are beautiful. Not every flower is my favorite, and you look better growing next to some than you do to others, as do I. Yet together we are astonishing. It takes our differences to create this effect.

So, when you do something that I imagine to be imperfect, I will remember that you are only reflecting back to me, my own beauty. I will thank you for reminding me. I will remember that we are necessary parts of the field, of the whole, of the one that is love.

Thank you for taking this journey with me. I love you unconditionally. You are beautiful.

Day 6

This quest is about noticing anger, sadness or any negative emotion and letting it pass on by. It is about separating ourselves from our ego.

It asks us to realize that WE run our emotions and not the other way around. It asks us to realize that with every reaction to an event or statement, we are declaring our choice. *Our choice.* Not the choice of the "other". Ours. We are running the show.

Emotions are responses to stimuli, of which there is an abundance. They do not dictate who you are.

You can feel sad because your lover has left and retain your connection to source. Your source is love. It is the basis of your power. It is what you are made of. The vibration of sadness will pass once you separate yourself from identification with it. If you hold on to it, it sticks to you and defines you in this dream.

Once you let it go, you will notice your power. You are more than abuse, poverty, a breakup, illness, anger or insult. You are divine. The truth is that you co-created the last upset to see clearly who you are NOT. You may have missed it before. Your partner in this co creation has gifted you with the opportunity to see it this time.

Don't miss it. Pay attention. You are at the controls and you know how to use the dials, even if others know how to "push your buttons".

The reason to withhold judgment is because you are coming now to love. This quest is drawing to its natural conclusion. You realize that you have been judging yourself. It is time to love yourself.

If you notice a judgment and it brings insight, that is great. If you notice a judgment and you are confused, don't despair. Let it go anyway and trust that insight will come. You may need a few more run ins with this particular judgment before you can identify it in yourself.

Trust your internal wisdom. It is there, beneath layers of guilt and anger and feelings of loss. You are finding something priceless, you are discovering your divinity.

The light that you are is waiting. It's been here, all along, like a candle burning beneath a basket. WE ARE UNCOVERING YOUR BRILLIANCE AND AS ONE, LIGHTING THE WAY FOR THE WORLD.

This is no small Quest, it is the ultimate Quest and you are leading the way. The light that you are is before me now, leading me home.

Day 7

I am surrounded by love. These Quests we are taking show me, beyond doubt, that we are one.

This is unity. The consciousness of the one that we are, is one force, one being, One. I feel you. Each of you is within me, as I am within each of you.

This is why it is a fruitless enterprise to fight another. You are fighting you, in another suit.

There are an infinite number of ways to live. There are an equally infinite number of ways to respond to life as it appears before you.

This is all set up by us, by you, by me. It has been overwhelmed with many outside forces to lure you into believing you must fight for what is right, what is good. Nothing could be further from the truth. YOU ARE THE TRUTH. IT IS TIME YOU REALIZE IT.

What feels good internally is in concert with your eternal

divinity. I will say that again. WHAT FEELS GOOD INTERNALLY IS IN CONCERT WITH YOUR ETERNAL DIVINE SELF.

That is where you want to stay. Hang out there, that feel good space, that happy place, that spot where your love is felt. From there you will exhibit your greatest power. You will know when you are there.

The most powerful thing you can do in your life is to take control of your emotions. Emotions are the fuel of creation. They energize your creative potential and make it possible for you to rapidly experience more of whatever you are feeling. Understand that this could be love or this could be fear.

Just feel good. This does not take anything more than a decision in your heart. It is a decision you will have to make over and over and over until it becomes the fabric of your life.

I love you. You and I are one. We have come to this place to remind each other of our brilliance. As we nudge each other into awareness, the field of love expands and becomes a world of love. That is unity consciousness. There is no force equal to the love that we are as ONE.

*Blasts from the Past

From Day 1

Those sparks were real and could be seen shooting off of my fingertips. Things like that were not uncommon at that point in time. It was August of 2011. There were frequent validations of my increasing extra-sensory abilities and strange happenings were common-place. This is not the place for those stories but suffice to say that life was showing up in magical & mysterious ways.

From Day 5

There are almost 500 of us. This is hard to believe, as our first quest was attended by less than 5 people, one of whom was me. That growth in numbers had occurred in 5 months' time. That is a true ripple effect and was amazing news. Our numbers had increased so quickly. For each one of us that began, there was that, multiplied by 100. Looking back, it seems as if, at this time, (2011) we all were feeling empty and yet realizing that the emptiness included a question. That question was "why?". It was followed by "what can we do about it?".

With the Quest, we attempted to find answers, and to find them together.

The truth

Prelude*

On this Quest, we will create a visceral experience of love. We'll do that with hugs. Whether mentally or physically, we will embrace ourselves until we can feel the love that we are.

Each day for seven days, upon waking, look in the mirror. Look into your own eyes.

Say "I love you."

Now, wrap your arms around yourself and squeeze. Don't let go until you can feel your love.

If, for some reason you would rather do this mentally, that's all right. Just close your eyes and imagine you giving you a loving embrace. Feel the love course through your body.

Now begin your day.

Welcome. Please follow along one day at a time.

This is not a race. Everyone wins on the Love Quest.

Day 1

This Quest for Love is a search. It is a search to remember the truth. You have come here on purpose. Each of you had some general plan before you incarnated here and as the designer of the plan, you know the specifics internally.

You have forgotten. It is ok, that too, is part of the plan – the forgetting. You set it up that way so that you'd believe this dream you are living. You'd never have to fake it – all emotional responses to the dramas in your life have been genuine. You believed you were broke, broken, beaten, mistreated, sad, abused, ill, alone...

You are on this Quest now because a part of you suspects a ruse. You have an inclination that the truth is very different from what you've believed up until now. You've heard about creation, there are many teachers. Yet this habit of belief pulls you. Again, and again you get caught in your own "stuff" and you feel bad. More "stuff" gets piled on, mixed now with some guilt (because you realize that on some level you are creating all of it), and – you forget the truth. You may not know what the truth is.

The truth is that it is and always has been YOU. As the starting and ending point of every moment in your life, you are the only creator.

What you think, you see, and what you feel, you become. Feel great and think love and the life that unfolds before you will be magical.

You've heard these words perhaps, yet without practical application they are meaningless. In the single act of absolute agape, every answer is given.

Love for no reason. Today and every day for the next seven days – appreciate yourself; be gentle with yourself, love yourself, hug yourself.

When the self-talk begins, gently talk back and say "Thanks, but I'm on a quest for only love today and those words are anything but. I love you. You need to stop now." Then mentally hug yourself.

You are terrific. You are perfect. The wisdom and power of the Creator exists in your every atom. The words you hear in your head do not support one such as you. They are not words you'd speak aloud, not to your worst enemy.

Take your own arms, wrap them around your shoulders and squeeze. Say "Thank you. I am so glad you are here." Send yourself some love. Lots of love. Nothing but love.

Love for no reason. It is unconditional self-love that is agape. Love of self is not a bad thing. It is the only thing. We are one.

Loving yourself will replenish you. It will empower you. As you disarm your objections with love, you will emerge whole and strong and clear. Your light will shine and I will be illuminated, we all will be brighter. The darkness and fear are no match for a world full of brilliance.

I love you. Thank you for your love and your beautiful perfection.

Day 2

Today we are going to talk about relationships.

You are on this Quest because of the single most important relationship in your life. Your relationship with yourself. It is not something we often think about in this context. We separate out our "luck" in love, and our feelings about ourselves. Nothing could be further from true.

You are surrounded with evidence for everything you believe. It shows up in every relationship. It starts with you and branches out to your parents, your friends, your children, your boss, your lovers, and the clerk at the store you just visited.

All relationships have one thing in common. That thing is YOU. Love, and its discovery and day to day function in your life, is how you realize who you are.

You are the essence of love. It springs from your very core. You cannot help but love in each interaction because to expect another force to spring from you is akin to expecting a different substance to emerge when something changes its own form.

A melting ice cube becomes water. It will never become anything else.

Do you understand? Each component of you, each relationship you have, is a way to express what it is you actually are – LOVE.

There is no greater or lesser relationship, all are equal. Some may be appreciated more than others yet that is simply preference and not a statement of value.

Realize how valuable you are and the others in your life will take note. That is how it works. "Luck" has nothing to do with love. What you give, (first to yourself), is what you get.

So today, give yourself another hug. Send yourself some love. Lots of love. Nothing but love. As a pebble in a pond, who knows just how far it will spread.

I love you absolutely.

Day 3

It is our third day. How are you doing? One of the favorite parts of our Quests is that I think about love continuously. Each day my world gives up ample opportunities for reflection. I was with many people yesterday, helping out at an event for my son's school. There was the usual joking around and pleasant camaraderie amongst the parents...and then something different. We got personal.

I am not sure what changed, yet our conversation became one of quiet honesty and sharing. The focus was unhappiness. I was struck by the desperation of this beautiful, upbeat woman when she said "I don't know what is wrong with me. I have this amazing husband, the best kids, I love my parents and I am not happy." Her eyes were filled with tears. Other women concurred and the men in the group sort of circled and listened without comment.

What I was thinking was "This is why there is a Love Quest." What I said was, "You have to love yourself. Until you do, it won't matter how many others love you." Everyone agreed yet no one knew how to do that.

She was speaking for all of us. There is a deep unhappiness that we attempt to fill with the love of others. We grow up believing on some level in the "happily ever after" as something that exists and that we should strive for. We set up our own lives to fit that mold in whatever fashion we choose, and then, wake up each day not feeling happy, and not knowing why.

The specifics of why may differ, but at the core there is fear; fear of not being good enough, not looking good enough, not loving enough or in the right way or the right people... it is fear. Fear is the opposite of love. Until the fear is released, the love cannot fill its place in your heart.

Loving yourself is a statement of self-worth. It is not arrogant to love yourself. It is necessary. You are unhappy because you don't feel good. You don't feel good because you don't like yourself. You have some sort of judgment about the worth of you. Do you deserve to be loved? Are you good enough?

Judgment has no place in love. You are here. You are love. You are perfect where you stand.

The fear you are feeling is the fear of your ego. Your ego is the personality you have created for this lifetime. It is not YOU. It is the role you are currently playing. It is temporary and will change. Your ego is not sure what role you are going to choose and so it hangs on with iron chains, holding you in place with fear. If you are afraid, you won't change, you will stay where you are, and your ego will lose nothing.

Don't fight your ego. Love your ego. Talk to your ego. Tell it that you understand yet you are not afraid anymore and it is time to do something new. You are going to love now. Only love.

Then hug yourself. Physically. A hug is a wonderful transference of energy. You can feel another when you hug them. Their energy becomes mixed with yours for a moment and you connect.

Connect with yourself. Feel the love that you are. Hold yourself and send yourself some love. You are beautiful. You are divinity. You are love.

Thank you for blessing my day. I love you.

Day 4

It is the fourth day of this Quest for Love. We are half way; midpoint on our journey.

Think about what a hug is. It is a transfer of energy. It is physically connecting; intentionally sending love. It is wonderful when given and yummy when received.

Here's the thing. In giving yourself a hug, you are validating your own worth. You are acknowledging the power of your own light. Love is what you are and *there is no greater evidence for that than when* **you are the only one in the room and you feel it.**

YOU FEEL LOVED BECAUSE YOU ARE LOVE.

Hug yourself. Really get into it. Wrap yourself in your own arms and don't let go until you feel it, until you know that you are loved and *oh so worth being loved.* Send the message of love right through your bones.

You have been thinking all along that you need love to come from outside in order to feel good. You are mistaken. It is always you from whom your love springs. There is no one else out there. Not really. We are all reflecting back for you, your deepest feelings.

You are looking at yourself. You are feeling from the world what you believe is truth within. You are worth loving. You are an actual piece of love and once you comprehend the source of love in your life, you will never be without it.

You see, we are all turtles, carrying with us all that we need, only we've been unaware. We've been searching and searching for a place to sink our heart into and call home; a place to feel safe and secure and loved; a place we could always count on. We have been trying to go home for such a long time and yet, home is in our own hearts. We have been hanging onto it the whole time. We never actually left.

Realize that everything you need, you have. See the love that you are and feel it. Know your truth. Once you do, your life will transform. You will see love reflected in every face, in each moment, in all interactions.

The truth is that you are love. Allow yourself the gift of you and feel your own light. You are brilliant. You are the one you are looking for.

Welcome home.

Day 5

We are more than half way through this journey. You have begun to "get" that "blame" is an often-used word that really has no place in relationships of any kind. There is never "fault". There is only choice. What you see is the picture you are choosing to construct. The filter of your personality cannot be removed from any situation. *You* are defining it as it is happening.

Quantum physicists have recently begun to clinically measure this effect, yet it has always been truth. As ONE (the collective), we all put the pieces there to work with, yet you, as a singular portion of the whole, interpret those pieces any way you choose.

This is why the future cannot be predicted, not precisely. There are movements in group consciousness that suggest probable outcomes... yet until you witness it, nothing has actually occurred.

Think about the power in these words. The power held by you. The power of your choice is the absolute power of the universe.

Our planet is undergoing a physical shift at roughly the same time that our mass consciousness is shifting. You are in control and are deciding with your focus just how destructive or life affirming these changes will be.

It is up to you. It always has been. Perhaps you have never known this, yet the past is irrelevant. What is important is every NOW.

Hold love as your focus and watch your world reflect it back to you in every instance. It may take practice and persistence but really, what else is there to do? It is as easy as changing your mind. It cost nothing and it is not necessary to move or change jobs or relationships. Just decide to see a world of your wildest dreams. Decide to love always.

Love for no reason. It is this act that will shift our consciousness to unity. This is the shift of the ages we've been hearing about.

The time is now.

There is no benefit gained from naming who's at fault or imagining negative or destructive scenarios. Your imagination and your focus are your most powerful tools.

Use them to imagine love.

Start with you. You are absolute brilliance. Your light has been hidden. No more. We know how beautifully bright you are and we want to bask in the glow.

Love yourself and you'll feel as if you plugged yourself in. You have. Source – yours, mine, and everyone's, is love. All you have to do is connect to it and you will re-charge.

Everything you need, you have right this very minute. It's like you've had this new toy for years, but never knew what it could do because you didn't have batteries for it.

You've got them now – they are right here and have been all along. Love yourself. Connect to your very source and see what you are capable of. You will amaze us all. We are waiting...

I love you absolutely.

Day 6

You are beginning to understand that love is not something you have to search for, as if it is lost, but that love simply is. Love is what you are. It is your life force and the source that enables you to exist here and now.

You only need to recognize it.

Love is a noun. It is you. It is me. It is us.

Love is *the ultimate power of the universe*. Appreciate what that means. Simply by loving, you can change the world.

We are one. A collective. An infinite gathering of light. We are made of the same stuff. Connected. As one drop of food color alters the container of liquid – the realization, or "waking up", of one of us changes all of us.

Love is contagious and contiguous. It is organic, in our very cells, and deeply rooted. You do not have to "drink the water" to the feel the change to love. It is seamless and happens regardless of it being noticed. All particles of water in the bucket are equally tinted when the single drop of dye is added, both those at the bottom and those at the top.

It is true that those nearby will be the first to notice your light, yet all will feel your illumination.

As a localized point of source energy, it all starts with you. Look at yourself – your hands, fingers, arms, torso, legs, and feet. Look in the mirror. This is YOU. You are a piece of infinity, sitting here right now, in an office or home or restaurant. How cool is that?

Now you may, out of habit, be noticing your supposed "imperfections" but I am here to tell you that *there are none*. Beauty is an assemblage of imperfections. Think of the difference between that field of wildflowers and that room of plastic ones. Do you understand?

There is nothing imperfect about who you are. This was your plan. If you are unhappy with the picture you see before you, change your mind and it has no choice but to follow suit.

You are a being sourced from divine energy. Nothing can top that. Remember this truth as you go about your life, your job and errands and family and all of it. Hold it within as a private treasure. Think about the truth of you, and smile. I will feel your smile here; we all will share in your happiness and it will multiply our own.

The one who you are waiting for is you. Right now. You are perfect where you stand. I can't wait to feel your love.

Day 7

Our Quest for Love is completed in linear time, yet in truth it always goes on. Now that you know the truth, there is no way to stop it. Love is everywhere. It is in the eyes of the one you saw in the mirror this morning. It is in the eyes of each person you engage with today.

Oh, they may not know it. They may have put on their "angry eyes" to fool you, but you know better. You know that beneath their costume of hurt is only love.

Each of us only wants love. We are swimming in a sea of love and so much of the time we've been riding above it, in our self-made boat of despair. It is time to jump in the water and stay afloat, buoyed by all that love. Love is holding us up.

Have you hugged yourself today? Do it now and validate the love that you have to give. Feel the love that is you. This feeling of love is what you are searching for, hoping for, striving to find. Give it to yourself. Once you do, you realize that you have been the source of it all along.

It begins in your very own heart. There are no reasons not to love. The heart is something available to all of us. We all have one, and they beat as one. More than seven billion hearts, all beating together, right this very minute, and you feel alone?

You are connected to me, to everyone reading these words, to everyone on this planet. You are connected.

It is time to acknowledge that connection in your every moment. There are no more excuses. You know how this works.

We are one. We can each participate in this shift to love/unity consciousness with our very own hearts. No special equipment is required, and we don't have to go anywhere or pay anyone to learn how. It is our natural state.

I know you may be sad, or ill, or frustrated, or broke, or angry or hurt or frightened. I have been all of those things and still struggle on occasion. I grew tired of my own drama and gave it up several years ago.

The hope for constant happiness kept me going when it was really dark. Some tiny spark of possibility whispered from the corner of my soul, saying *"you can get through this and it will be sooooooo worth it. You can't imagine the wonders you will discover and they never end."*

I am so glad I hung on. Now, I get to be here with you. I hope you do as well (hang on). Life is amazing and I get it now. I get the amazing part. I get it because I have uncovered it. It has always been here. Now I know the truth. It can be seen in my own eyes and in the eyes of everyone I meet.

The amazing part of life is love. Since love is what you are, at your very core, the amazing part of life is YOU.

I am so very grateful to have had this opportunity to love you. Thank you.

I love you absolutely.

*Blasts from the Past

From the Prelude

Here is the invitation as sent in September of 2011:

"This is a Quest for Love. In the seven days it lasts, you will be asked to look for it. You know what it looks like because you know what it feels like. It feels true.

There is nothing else that feels like love. It is familiar, strong and deep. You recognize it. What I have come to understand is that it is everywhere.

I stood in the middle of Chicago the other day and felt it hundreds of times, from complete strangers. Over and over, with every hug, I felt it. It went right through me. It was palpable. It was love. **

It is not because we were lovers or family or from the same religion or country. It is not because of our looks or our clothes or our money. It is because we are one, and the one that we are, is love.

Love does not need a reason.

You are perfect. Each day of this Quest, you will imagine being hugged by you. This is a hug with intention. This is a hug that says: "For no other reason, just because you are here, I love you. I recognize who you actually are and you are wonderful."

You will be asked to visualize. Envision a you other than this current version, (this could just be a different set of clothes), wrap your arms around yourself and squeeze. Send your energy right through yourself. Find the love that you are. Feel your own truth.

Your truth is mine as well. We are love. Every one of us. The realization of this truth is the shift we have all been waiting for.

Loving yourself is paramount.

You are looking for that feeling, the one you recognize, the one that is familiar and goes deep. You are reaching for that precise emotion when you think about you. Not because you just did something special or because you look good or because someone else told you they loved you, but because you love you, without condition.

It is love for no reason that will change your life, your vibration and this world.

We are one. Once you love you, knowing yourself completely, you will love everyone without condition. Not because they believe as you do, but just because.

Just love yourself. I love you absolutely.

See you on the Quest."

** That same month, a few of us held a "Hug Quest" in the city of Chicago, by the "Bean". It was remarkable and wonderful. We stood there with signs saying "Hug Quest" hanging around our necks and hugged whoever was willing. This turned out to be a surprising number of people.   Lilou Mace' showed up for a few moments because she was in town. She hugged us as well.

Fear

Prelude

We'll be looking at fear this week. Fear is the opposite of love. How does it show up in your life?

Fear has many names. They include impatience, annoyance, doubt, tension, anger, violence, destruction, frustration, sarcasm, and insult. You get the idea.

Each morning for 7 days, wake up and look into your mirror. Look deeply into your own eyes.

Say "I love you."

Say "You are stronger than anything or anyone that tries to tell you otherwise."

Hug yourself and feel the strength of your love. You can do this mentally or physically upon waking, and then again at any point when you feel that reinforcement is necessary.

Welcome. Please follow along one day at a time.

This is not a race. Everyone wins on the Love Quest.

Day 1*

Hello and welcome to this Love Quest.

I find myself overwhelmed with numerous responsibilities. What I couldn't figure out was why. Why now.

Until I figured it out. Now I understand that I have given myself this incredible gift. The gift of truth, all wrapped up in fear. I have since remembered who I am. I then remembered who you are. You are so much more than what your eyes are seeing.

You are love. You are eternal. You are multi-faceted and you exist beyond your wildest expectations. If, like mine, your life seems to be screaming at you with dense and numerous responsibilities, know that yes, they are there, and they are no more important than the other things in your life, such as finding peace within, maintaining your closest relationships, sharing and giving the love that you are.

You are not too busy to love. Not ever.

I love you. Now I really get that the reason for this Quest, as with all the Quests, is my own evolution and growth. We are one, and I hope that by sharing with you here, you will be assisted on your journey. I know that I am. Thank you for sharing your time with me.

I look forward to connecting with you tomorrow.

Day 2

Welcome to our second day on this Quest. I am fairly bursting with things to write about... Yesterday has started an avalanche of love.

Our journey is one of exploration. We are looking at love and considering the notion of fear. What place does *fear* have in our lives? I will submit here that it may look different for each of us, but it feels identical. It feels like *not love*.

Now, for a moment understand that love feels the same for each of us. Love is truth. It matters not from where it springs. It may be felt while looking at an infant or a puppy or a sunset or your Beloved. It may be felt in an embrace with a complete stranger. It may be experienced during prayer or meditation. It may be passionate or joyful or serene or peaceful. Words describe it differently, but it is a universal, organic feeling. It runs right through you. It can be judged but it cannot be denied. It does not go away. What is true is true under any condition. It exists. Truth and love are really one and the same. Both define YOU.

This is a dream you are having. It is a field of awareness, of consciousness if you will, that exists *only because you say it does.* Only because you believe that it does. It is not "real" in the sense that it exists eternally. It does not. *(But YOU do.)*

This (life) is a thought you are having. There are others who are having similar thoughts and that is why this plane of existence is here – *there was a decision to create in such a way that the experience would be absolutely, purely felt and completely actualized.* In order to do that – you slowed down your vibration enough so that you became, or appeared to become, dense physically.

As such, the dense, physical vibrational being that you appeared as, could have all sorts of experiences – hot and cold, happy and sad, comfortable and painful, healthy and ill, powerful and fearful.

The field grew in complexity with time and interaction. There is no limit to what this body you appear as now is capable of doing, having or being. It's a dream and you are merely a thought form - in a dream you are having.

Understand, truly, that the emotions you are feeling all spring from this dream self – they are made up. Play things. When you are done playing with them, you will put them away and play with something else.

YOU will do that, no one else. There is no one else "out there". It's all you.

Fear is a very compelling play thing. It engages us fully. It takes our mind off other things, and that is the reason it exists.

We have come to a place in our evolution as a species that we see clearly. We see what fear is and what it represents. It is not a threat. It is merely an emotion. We can have fear (*or any emotion*) just as long as it serves our intent, and then we can choose something else. Fear is not real. What is that acronym - False Evidence Appearing Real? There is such truth in this acronym.

There is no fault in being afraid, but you are bigger than anything you are afraid of. YOU ARE ETERNAL. YOU ARE LIFE ITSELF. YOU ARE LOVE ABSOLUTELY.

Fear only exists for as long as you say it does. It is time to say you are done with "afraid". You have bigger things to take care of now. There are people to love, (**you first,** and then everyone else) - *there is a planet/consciousness to shift.* You have much to do and you can do it from the place you carry with you always. You can do it from your heart.

We are all waiting. We are waiting for you to show us back to love, to guide the way to truth. There is no longer a reason to be afraid. You have come to this place as a piece of perfection, and you exist just precisely as you planned to. You are doing a great job. Nice work, you master creator you. You are beautiful.

I love you. Thank you for sharing this time with me.

Day 3*

Hello. Welcome to day #3. I am so happy you have joined us here. Thank you.

This Quest will stare fear right in the eyes and absorb it. Today, we begin to look at what sort of havoc it can wreak in our lives. There are so many things to be afraid of – they all boil down to a perception of loss.

This is a universal lens. In your life/house/body there are probably some requirements you have not fulfilled, constant reminders of imperfection/incompleteness/unworthiness. They are lies. You have believed them long enough. You can set it up as I have, and force yourself to remove them, or you can bravely stare them down and tell them (lovingly) to leave. They no longer suit you.

Each is a symptom – a symptom of loss. We will have to let them go. They (these requirements) no longer fit us. We are ready to remove this filter of density. It has caused us to see 3D as all there is, all important and burdensome and AT CAUSE. This filter is a lie, covering the truth of our perfection.

Realize that as you are now seeing the filter for what it is, it will ramp up its intensity, as if to say *"really?", "so, you think I'm not real, do you?", "well, let me prove to you how 'real' I can be."*.

Don't believe it. You are testing yourself. The tougher the tests, the greater your satisfaction will be once you pass.

All of our life is creation. What kind of life do we want? By allowing old repetitive thoughts to fill our brains, we are creating. By meditating, we are creating. By walking in the sunshine, we are creating. By loving, we are creating.

Insist on truth. You know what that is. Love yourself in every moment. You are divine. Divinity is not negated because of a messy home, a few extra pounds or mistakes or unpaid bills or wrong turns. Divinity is truth. The truth cannot be denied.

Love that which you are - in every moment, every outfit, each circumstance, all of your chores and every relationship. The power in you is beyond what you have ever realized. It is time to realize it now.

You are here to realize the truth and help me recognize it as well. Together we are here to shift an entire planet and transform our consciousness from fear to love. It begins in our homes – time to get to work.

I love you. Thank you.

Day 4

Hello again and welcome to the 4th day.

Today I am left with an internal quietness as well as a question, what do I do now that there are no more excuses? I have been afraid of that question, run out of excuses, and can no longer hide behind unmet requirements.

Fear is an interesting emotion. It is fully engaging and the perfect excuse. It works every time. If you have children, you may even have used fear as a tool in keeping them safe from whatever imagined "harm" could befall them.

Fear has kept us quiet and disempowered, in our homes with our doors locked. Fear has stopped us from taking chances. Fear has limited our love. Fear is not based on truth. Fear is based on the illusion of loss.

Realize that if you are afraid to do something because you may look bad, that this "you" that looks bad *is only one version of you – the "right this moment" you.*

In truth, the others who may be witnessing that version will have their own story, that they are much more worried about than yours. They are just as afraid as you. It doesn't matter who they are or where they live or how beautiful, rich, poor or alone they are. They are afraid.

We are afraid that someone or something is going hurt us, and we will lose something because of that hurt. It could be our money, health, image or loved one. Fear is not real. What we are afraid of is loss.

It is time to come from love instead of fear. It starts with us. By looking in the mirror each day and just loving the "you" that looks back, you are looking beyond this dream. You are doing what you came here to do. You are loving, and you are able to love inside of any circumstance.

You came here to love. That is the point of your life. You have your own style and your own story, but beneath it all, it is your purpose to create. To create from love, not fear.

We see out there a world that has been created from fear. The only enemies are in our head. If we see everyone as versions of us, and we love ourselves, we will see clearly and act accordingly.

Love who you are. You are perfect and whole and brilliant. If you don't have the right answer to whatever is going on in your life, you will find it. YOU will fix your life. It is not up to anyone else. Removing a symptom does not fix anything. It merely makes room for another symptom.

My own home may be clean now, but there are lists upon lists to put in its place and keep me stuck. I am lovingly letting them go. Nothing gets created until that happens. None of this is real. There is nothing to hang on to.

Only love is real. You are love. That is what you hang on to. The love. Your light. It is shining each day and lighting the way for the rest of us. It is more powerful than any imagined darkness. Your love, your light, is truth. It is the only truth.

I love you so very much. Thank you for being here.

Day 5

Hello. We are on our 5th day. How are you feeling?

I have been thinking about love and fear and what it is that we want. What draws us to each other? To this Quest? And conversely, what keeps us away?

Life and love are about evolution. We are never standing still. Each person/soul with whom you engage is a part of your plan, in your life by prior agreement between both of you. We each have something to gain from this moment now.

Recognition of another soul with whom you connect may not always feel good. It often doesn't, but it is always deeply familiar. That "other" who really gets to you, offers you an opportunity to see yourself. Chances are - you "get" to them as well. This is a perfect universe, and what you feel at one end of the stick is felt at the other end, no exceptions.

What is done about the feeling or how that feeling is defined is determined individually and by life path. Yet, what is felt is always felt mutually, guaranteed. If another causes you a gut level response, you can be sure they feel it too.

This is not universally appreciated. Where the confusion comes in, is when each of us defines what the feeling signifies — it always signifies love. Love is what we are at the core and where we connect. Always the core component is the same. Love is the unifying element.

If you feel strongly affected by someone, you know them on a level that perhaps you don't see. This is only one "dream" of thousands you have had, and as pieces/fragments of Source, you have always been connected and have played many roles together. These "others" are in your life to assist you as you are in theirs to assist them; we have a common goal.

Helping another will always help you because the other IS you. There are no small moments. There are no insignificant acts of love.

To unite and love universally will be possible when first we LOVE. Love yourself; then to love all others will pour forth from you as breath. You will extend no greater effort to love another, to love ALL others, when it is realized that you too are worthy, deserving and perfect.

Every part of you is worthy; all blemishes, mistakes and perceived faults. "God doesn't make junk", is a simple truth uttered by an angel I had the privilege to know and love in this lifetime.

You are God personified and each part of you exists as a complete expression of divinity. God would not, COULD NOT be, without you.

Do you understand?

As the hand is not complete without the thumb, God needs you for complete expression of Creation. You have come here so that you could show the rest of us a piece of the whole that we COULD NOT SEE without you to show us. You are doing a fine job.

Thank you.

Day 6*

Good morning. I have been thinking about fear. There is so much going on right now, both personally and globally. I am seeing this Quest as an opportunity to explore what for so many of us has become "business as usual".

Here's the thing, there is a fine line between noticing the differences and holding an opinion about them while labeling them. Life simply exists here as a platform in which to experience ourselves. True non-judgment is a very rare thing to discover in another human. It signifies an evolved soul.

Not judging does not mean living without preferences. I do not enjoy popcorn. I do not think there is something wrong with my children because they love popcorn. Perhaps, *if I was unsure of my decision* about popcorn, I would ridicule popcorn lovers and make them wrong for their choice. Perhaps I would attempt to get them to come over to my side, the side where all the intelligent, popcorn haters sit. This would bolster my self-esteem, my belief in the "rightness" of my popcorn beliefs.

There are no "right" popcorn decisions, just as there are no "right" ways to live your life. All is choice. When you understand, absolutely that each choice you make is only a choice for a singular moment and nothing more, you become much less attached to the choices of others. Each life is a singular moment, filled with decisions/choices. Freedom is non-attachment. Freedom is love.

Each lifetime chosen provides a different approach, another way to experience creation. This is why there is no cause for fear. Fear only exists because you believe you can lose something – your life, your reputation, your money, your love – you cannot lose what isn't real.

What is real is you. It is love. Love truly felt is something never lost. It is something no one can take from you. It exists as truth.

You know it as such simply because YOU exist. You are here. At your core you are love. The joy, the passion, the thrill of loving is so absolute because it is your very source. YOU are the source of your love.

This is the thing, the only thing really, that I have wanted to share in these Quests. Loving yourself is not a greeting card sentiment, it is a necessity. It is the source of your power. You will freely live, with a head full of preferences, secure in the knowledge that each choice is okay. You are not defined by the choices you make, the size of your bank account or your clothes. You are defined by the one element. It is the same for everyone else. It is love.

Everyone is love. You may not prefer the company of them all, and that is okay, that preference does not make them evil or you wrong. *Both of you are perfect.* Accepting yourself where you are will yield the ripest fruit and the most powerful, nourishing life.

Once you do, you will see the love in me, and in the rest of us. We are waiting for you to show us the love that we are. This is what you have come to do.

Thank you for taking this Quest with me. I love you.

Day 7*

Hello there. This Quest seemed to move very quickly, I am surprised this is the last day. Time seems to be moving faster now; I think science verifies this, so it is not my imagination.

Time is an interesting illusion. It feels so very real here and it allows for a great deal of contrast, fear and interaction with each other. On the road, we can literally "crash" into another vehicle because one or both did not move quickly enough. We have seen others; perhaps we have been someone, who pushes ahead in line because of this idea of not wanting to be "late". Afraid of wasting "time" we barely look at each other in the stores and streets we frequent. We are all in a hurry. A few kind words can seem like a waste of "time". Wow.

Fear does that. It creates in us the illusion of needing to be someplace else or with someone else that is more important. There is not "more" important. We are one. We are important.

I notice that at either end of the spectrum of linear years of life, time seems irrelevant. A young child will spend just as long as she pleases watching a ladybug crawl up her tiny arm – to her absolute delight. An older person will take a moment for a few words and a warm smile while shopping, often to the annoyance of the much younger person in line behind them.

The very, very young are closer to Source and the older have a lifetime of years behind them. Both perspectives afford an understanding that what matters *is* each moment, every life, and the chance for their full expression.

What matters is love. There is no reason to fear.

Fear can be expressed as need or worry or anxiety. There is nothing here but you. There is no one else but me. WE ARE ONE. As the boundaries dissolve and we begin to see oneness, our fears will dissipate.

It starts with you because you are the only thing there is. All else is a reflection, so that you could experience life...a reflection of YOU.

Loving yourself is paramount. *There is no blame or fault or blemish or action that creates a reason not to love.* Blame or fault or imperfections are pretend. They are costumes worn to experience results of creative efforts. Sometimes we make something and then decide it wasn't what we wanted. At that point we need a new decision; it can be tricky to figure out how to fix it so that it again pleases us. This is the reason we are here. We came for the challenge.

We are fixing our creations. WE ARE IN THE PROCESS OF STARTING OVER. We do this every moment. Every thought is a creative endeavor. We choose with each one, what we are creating. We declare with each one, who we are.

We began this Quest searching for love. We are still searching, not because we did not find it, but because in each new moment, LOVE IS RE-DEFINED. We are not static. We are in the process of evolution. As we appreciate and love, we grow and see differently.

New perspectives show up and they do not mean you were wrong yesterday, they mean you are always right. It is true in each moment that you are love. It is true right now that you are perfection. The next time you look in the mirror tell yourself thank you. Thank yourself for your willingness to engage. You are here. You are willing to love. You are sharing your light with me, with us, and because of you, this is a brighter place.

Thank you. Your willingness to love, your perfection and your wisdom just fills me up and carries me forward. Because of you, there is hope and there is love and there is a global shift in consciousness. You are awesome. I love you.

*Blasts from the Past

Day 1

This was our 9th Quest for Love. It was almost cancelled because of what I perceived to be a lack of linear time. This was actually perfect, and what I eventually saw as a gift. I had been afraid. Afraid of meeting responsibilities and meeting them to my own satisfaction. As this Quest is about fear, well, it was synchronistic and fueled this Quest with insights.

Day 3

This example of fear sounds sort of silly, in retrospect. Yet keeping a "cluttered" mind prevents introspection, which is a part of the motivation for it; avoidance. Clutter has so many costumes and they are typically not earth-shattering or life-defining ones.

"I have today, a day of chores in front of me. These include my every day, clean the bathroom sort of chores as well as another job; the perfect chore to be completed mid-Quest. It is one that has been building for years. There is no doubt that this was perfectly timed. It has to do with fear. It is a chore I have been dreading for a very long time.

I am an artist in my heart and organization is not my strong suit (to put it mildly). I also homeschool. I have a table full of papers and books and notes and records that need organization and a place to be. I have put this off for TWO YEARS. They have only been multiplying. Now, this weekend, I have no choice. They must be moved. There is construction being done in my basement and they must go in order for the workmen to get the job done. The time is now. There is no other option.

By holding on to this chore, my head has been full. Avoidance has been easy; I have too much to do. I have had too much to do for TWO YEARS... I have been afraid.

What will happen if I let this fear go? What will my head feel like with all that empty space? What will my life look like if I remove this lens of "unmet requirements"? Who will I be?"

Day 4

At the time, I delivered medical prescriptions to people who couldn't leave their homes to pick them up. This was through a local drug store.

The folks I delivered to were isolated due to illness, poverty, wealth or simply fear. I found that the people with the least in material things offered up the most in friendship and conversation; they were more open as a rule. The most beautiful homes were often locked down in more ways than one; they kept the world out of sight and mind, deliberately. Here was the comment that was made on this day, a reference to this job.

"One of my jobs brings me in contact with people from all walks of life, the very, very rich (the 1% everyone is occupying about), the very, very poor and the in between. I talk to and help, all of them. I have come to understand that it doesn't matter who you are or where you live, you are afraid of something. Mostly, we are afraid of the same thing."

Day 6

This was a time when "Occupy Wall Street" was happening worldwide.

The following comments refer to that.

"In the world, there are many thousands "occupying", declaring dissatisfaction with things the way they have been. Things are changing on so many levels. If I accept that we are making this all up, then I must also see that, as a collective, we are moving things around a bit - right now. We are finding a voice. We are challenging institutions and on the brink of taking control of not only our money, but our lives. I don't know that this has ever *happened world-wide, and it feels like an important step towards unity consciousness, towards empowerment.*

Personally, I realize that for unity to exist as a force, I must stop seeing separators. When I look at anything, I have noticed how my immediate reaction is to categorize it, label it even. Thoughts of "other" do not serve my intent for oneness. In order for a shift in consciousness, I must stop separating out the wealthy 1% as evil, the old as helpless and the young as incapable. I must stop separating, period. "

Day 7

Another reference to the worldwide Occupy movement:

"The entire movement of oneness is occurring all over the planet. In small towns and large cities, we are coming together as one. The reason this is happening is in no small part because of you. You may not be there physically, but energetically you are creating an atmosphere of unity."

Unity

Prelude*

Welcome to our Quest for love. Each day for 7 days you will find that love in your own eyes. As you look there, you will begin to notice the boundless, limitlessness of that love. It is the goal of this Quest to catch a glimpse of the possibilities found there.

Wake up and find yourself in your mirror. Do this each morning for one full week.

Smile once you do. There you are.

Say "Hello there. I love you."

Keep watching.

You will notice a bit of anxiety... what is it you are looking for? How long before it shows up?

It has shown up. Look deeper. It peeks out behind your discomfort, and peers around the sides of requirements. It is you and there are no borders holding you in now. This is love without condition; your core. It is this deep well from which your essence springs.

Welcome. Please follow along one day at a time.

This is not a race. Everyone wins on the Love Quest.

Day 1*

Hello.

Unity is an idea we have never held as a collective. It is one we reserve for family and loved ones, maybe nations and religions. We have held that "we are one" when we pray the same, sleep in the same house or share the same last name. While each idea is wonderful, it misses a whole lot more wonderful. It is what we are missing that I would like to explore together.

It is perhaps easy to be one with an idea on your laptop or mobile device. You agree, it sounds good to you, you believe it is true. What is not so easy is being one in your every day. The people you live with are your greatest teachers. You have chosen them to show you what you need to see. You have chosen perfectly. This does not mean you are enjoying your choice at the moment.

Getting the idea of unity means living it in this physical life – it means not seeing everyone else as "other". It means acceptance and it means power. Your power is not diminished when you recognize the strength of another, it is multiplied.

Oneness means seeing all others as different expressions rather than separate creatures. It does not mean taking on every tragedy or cause or idea. It means no judgment. You may not prefer a certain genre of music – that does not make it bad or immoral, it just makes it different. *In this vast field of creative expression, there exists every possibility.*

We came to experience all of them. Since we can't do that all at once, we split up and each took a different role. I experience myself through each emotion I feel when I watch, listen to or otherwise participate in your life.

We are love. If I understand that on a visceral level, it can become a challenge to function. Waves of love course through my physical self and I perceive it as overwhelming. I suspect though, that what I am feeling is truth. I suspect that the power of the love that knocks me literally off my feet exists as a contrast to the force of the negative polarity I have lived in – until now.

It was meant to feel that good. I am not sure about a constant orgasmic state, but something akin to that. We are LOVE. We are ONE. If we give up what separates us, there is no reason not to smile. This is our playground. We came to try every ride.

It sounds too good to be true because we have never experienced it as true. Until now, we have not been able to. This shift, the one we are making, is the kind of "hang on to your hats" sort of change. It will require constant awareness. We cannot hang back and wait for someone else to fix it up before we jump in. We are the ones we are waiting for.

The time to jump in is now, and we don't have to go anywhere. We can do it within. It begins, and it ends, with love.

Love yourself. You are ok. You are right where you are supposed to be in this very moment. Every inch of you is doing what you so brilliantly decided to do.

Once you accept the perfection of YOU, you will stand in your power. You will see that being surrounded by others who seem very different from you is actually ok too. They cannot take away the love that you are. You have come here now to join them, me, and us - and realize the power in unity.

We cannot do it alone. Isolation feels safe yet it is not. It feels lonely, regardless of how we justify it. We need to connect physically, with our families, our neighbors, our world. This is why we came. We cannot escape the fact that we are actually connected. We have come now to demonstrate what that looks like in a physical world.

There is so much to consider, the potential for unity or polarity exists in every thought we have. Let's think "oneness" and see what changes.

Thank you for taking this journey with me. I love you.

Day 2

Hello on our second day.

This day feels very different from yesterday... there was an energetic tension that was palpable and demonstrated all around me then. Everyone I spoke with had something to say about being extremely tired or agitated or upset to some degree. I believe it has to do with these rapid evolutionary shifts we are all participating in. The vibratory field in which we live is changing for us all. How we experience the change is individual. It is comforting to know we are in this together, this shift is OUR shift.

As it is OURS, it is time we take command of it. This is not something that is happening TO us, it is something that we are calling forth. This is a distinction we need to keep in our hearts. WE CHOSE THIS. We are here now, doing whatever we are doing, by choice. This is an important distinction. It is easy to get caught up in dialogue, and act as if someone else is doing this to us. Someone who must be fought, or at the very least, blamed.

Until we take responsibility for every part of our life, we will not understand the truth. The truth is that you and I are not lesser than any other force. We are the power of creation. I create my life and you create yours, and together we have participated in every facet of life that exists.

We are ONE; One force, One light, One love.

In order to successfully command this steering wheel, we must be free of judgment. It is self-judgment that will hold us back and halt our progress.

I have to start with me. I have to love myself. If I love myself, I will not falter or hide or doubt or hesitate. I will emerge whole and shining bright so that you may be illuminated. You will do the same.

If I am love, then there is nothing I cannot accomplish. If I am perfect, I have no reason to fear. If I hold the power of creation, then I know that anything that comes up is not beyond me. I can learn anything. I only have to believe.

Part of this change is the lifting of control off of what we have been told is truth. We know better now. WE KNOW WHO TO TRUST AND IT IS US. It is time to hold yourself straight with your head high and believe that you can do anything. You may not know how today, but you can find out and do it tomorrow.

Anything is possible because YOU ARE DIVINITY. **You hold the key to a seamless and loving transition to oneness... It is your heart.**

Just love. It starts inside. You are ok. You may act weird or silly or angry or hurt or unsure but that is just pretend. Somewhere inside you know the absolute brilliance that is you. You are a reflection of all of life, a creator of every moment, a radiant and powerful light that we all need so very much to see.

Just love. It is what we want from you, when all is said and done. Look with loving eyes on whatever is going on and you will know what to do next. You are here now to do just that.

Thank you. I am so grateful for your light, and your love.

Day 3

I have so many thoughts about unity and this shift in awareness
we are experiencing...

Here is what I have come to believe. I have spent countless hours
on this search for healing, enlightenment, consciousness,
knowledge, recovery. Regardless of name, it is all the same thing
– self-improvement. I believe I have been misunderstanding the
search. I no longer feel as if I need to be improved.

I believe that what I need is to accept who I am right now. In the
denial of ME, I have come very far from love. I hear many words
around the idea of denial, and they sound like re-programming,
de-programming, replacing ... and then they speak of adopting
some new and now way to fix what has been wrong all this time.

We do not need to be fixed. We need to be loved.

We need only love ourselves. As extensions of the ONE, everyone
else will fall right in line and love us as well. It is a great disservice
to assume that you are broken or wrong. You are not wrong.

Whatever you have thought, said or done is first of all in the past
and not really here any longer. Secondly it was thought, said and
done with the best information you had at the time. This is why

they say hind sight is always 20/20. **We move ever forward. We do not have a reverse gear because the past no longer exists.**

There are many teachers in this time of change. The greatest wisdom you will discover is the wisdom you UNCOVER. It is within.

We are eternal beings of light who have slowed down just enough to experience ourselves physically. It is extraordinary, this life on planet earth. That is why we are here. It is time now to enjoy the good parts.

Our habits of response have held us in patterns that may or may not facilitate our forward movement. It is not that those habits need to be labeled as wrong or bad or negative, it is that they need to be accepted. They are a part of the magnificence of you. Every part is necessary for the ONE to be complete. Every part is vital. Every part is depending on every other part in order to unite.

Love yourself. If there is a thought or feeling or action or re-action that you see does not serve you, accept it and absorb it and move ahead to do something else. Hating any part of you will not serve the idea of ONE LOVE. Every part is essential and needs to be loved. No judgment means no judgment, period.

I remember thinking when my children were very young how frustrating it was that they were not more upset when corrected for something they had done (this was something that I had undoubtedly decided was "wrong", sigh...). They were not particularly sorry or sad, and pretty much just listened politely, and then continued playing. Now I see that their self-esteem was perfectly intact. They did not define themselves by their actions, they knew who they were. It was me who was mistaken. Good thing they didn't listen very well.

I am not saying this will be easy, yet I have come to believe it is necessary. Agape is unconditional self-love. There is not one other person on this planet who knows you as well as you do. You MUST love the you that you are. By doing so, you will demonstrate for me how best to love you as well.

I will learn from you, how to love you. I need to see you love yourself so that I can love myself. Once you do, and I do, there will be nothing but love. The light that we are is dimmed by judgment. It is time to disconnect the dimming switch. Then the light will always be on, and all that we will feel from each other is love.

We are love. There are no longer any reasons not to be the love that we are. Unconditional means without condition. For me that means a great many things need still to be forgiven. In order to do so, I will see what they are and then gently set them down. They are like museum pieces, perhaps interesting but no longer part of who I am today. I am not disowning who I am, but celebrating her, all of her.

Without all of my past I could not be where I am. Where I am is pretty incredible. I love each of you so very much, you lift me up and for that I am honored. Thank you for joining this Quest.

Day 4

We are half way there. Today marks the midpoint on our Quest to Love.

I have been thinking about so many facets of our journey... fear and truth and love and division and oneness and us, which brings me right back to love.

The idea of "separate" pervades our life.

Each day I drive past a church that is right now announcing "Vespers for the faithful departed". My thought is always – "What about the *unfaithful* departed???"

We cannot help but see ourselves as different. The media, the government, and society as a whole, divides us so that we can be sold to, marketed, defined and controlled. It is time to define ourselves.

We do not need to be told the possibilities for our lives, *we need to discover them* and choose what serves us. This is not a simple thing for a race that has been more or less a "slave race". We WANT someone to take care of us, and to tell us right from wrong. The belief in a higher source is present in every doctrine. The notion of worship was taught from the very beginning.

What the Quest is searching for is truth, and that cannot be taught, it can only be known. There is a difference in *believing* something is true (Santa Claus) and *knowing a truth* (love). You may learn that it is wrong to love someone because of your current age or sex or nationality or religion, but that will not change the truth that is known in your heart.

Our internal conflict is a created falsehood. It is our ego-self that is acting out an agenda. It does not mean anything about the truth of our divinity.

We are the truth, the light and the ONE. We are love; beings of infinite power and wisdom, experiencing many different facets of existence while walking around on planet earth, eating, sleeping, working and loving.

It doesn't matter what we look like or what church we do or don't belong to. It matters that we love. Some of us will be beautiful, some handicapped, some rich, some poor, some unknown and others recognized worldwide; we are the same.

I am so very tired these last few days, I am changing internally. At a core level I am morphing. This shift we are going through is not linear and it is not experienced the same by each of us. It may feel differently for you, yet the energetic changes are real and they are happening now.

It is not business as usual, so don't blame yourself for wanting to rest more, or play more or relax more. This is an organic change happening in all parts of your body, spirit, mind and heart — it is happening in your entire life. The parts of you that are changing have an effect on all the other parts of you as well. It is never just one thing. YOU ARE ONE.

Take a deep breath and remember that you chose here and now to participate. You came to experience oneness, the actualization of truth in a very dense place that has existed for many thousands of years in duality. Your presence is necessary for us all.

Your love is vital and what you came to contribute can only be given by YOU. You are unique and brilliant and a perfect version of love.

This is no small thing. It is wild and science fiction like and amazing and FUN. Embrace the change and each and every facet of the experience. It is the shift of the ages and YOU ARE HERE. You have a front row seat, actually. Whether you noticed or not, you are also holding the steering wheel. Push the pedal to the metal and enjoy the ride.

I love you. This is one incredible dream we are having. Thank you for sharing your time with me. WE are ONE.

Day 5*

Hi. Today I would like to talk about Love. It is the subject of this Quest, and it is such a powerful thought.

Love is what you are. This idea is one you have all heard before. The realization of the truth of that sentence will allow the full actualization of your divinity.

Love is the force of creation, force in the way that it emanates out *from* – not in the act of forcing your will or desires artificially onto another. Force is the only word (*I can think of*) that depicts the strength and action that love is.

Love springs from your very core – not a gentle trickle as in a stream, but powerfully and constantly, as in the Hoover Dam. It flows through you and from you. Gone unchecked, it would be obvious to the world. You would be surrounded in an always field of smiles and kindness and compassion. This is *you.*

We have never seen walking, talking, pure love unleashed. The leash that holds us back is fear. Without that leash fastened, we would realize our truth. We are the power of creation. The force in that is beyond any outside ability to control. It can only be commanded from within, realized and accepted by you, as *you.*

Love is who you are. It is an unstoppable force. It is not that you are getting something from somewhere or someone else; it is that you are removing the blinders to your own light.

You don't need to shield yourself any longer. You only need to shine.

There is no one to fear, we are the same. I am you, you are me, and we are one.

Globally, we are realizing our oneness. We are evolving as a collective. This is just so cool.

Just love. The force in that is immeasurable and always available. The steering wheel has always been ours to command. It is just that we were *"asleep at the wheel"*. We have woken up. Now, to be awake in every moment, that is the trick.

I love you. Thank you. See you tomorrow.

Day 6*

It is your sixth day.

You are the shift. WE are the shift. The consciousness is increasing its vibration and although I cannot point to a specific dimensional level, I can feel the change.

This is what love does. Love is the most powerful force we have. It is you.

Love is what is keeping your heart going and propelling your life as this third dimensional soul you came to be, as well as the next dimensional being you are evolving towards.

To discover self-love is a singular treat. It is akin to getting the one thing you really wished for, but never expected because it was just TOO big, and TOO fantastic to be real.

It is real. Love and bliss are synonymous with you.

There is no other truth. Once uncovered, the force of the light that shines from you will light everyone. This is the halo you see drawn on so many paintings of your divine masters. It is a depiction of their light. They realized their truth and the light that they were, was palpable and visible.

We have been born to a time when much of what we have been told up until now is untrue. You don't have to do anything special to get this love that you are. It is not a case of being worthy or deserving. Everyone has access, and everyone gets it for free. There are no exceptions.

You have come to realize your truth. Love exists because you exist. Creator desired life and that one thought is YOU, standing there, desiring life in whatever fashion suits you.

The truth of love is that it is. Love is. You are. WE ARE. ONE.

Day 7

It is with utmost respect I come to you today, for each of you and your willingness to engage in this exploration of your deepest held beliefs. It is an honor.

I have come face to face with much about myself. At the core of all that I struggle with, is one thing. It is fear. I have come to understand that fear is the basis for my every action. It is not truth that propels me, it is fear.

I spoke of the halo painted around enlightened individuals and the visible light and palpable love that emanated from them. This is only possible when fear is eradicated completely.

We have been taught to be afraid. Our parents were afraid. Their parents were afraid and on it goes to the very first human. We come from fearful beginnings. Now, in this birth of a new age, we are starting again. This time, we emerge fearless.

This is not a small thing. The ramifications for fearless living do not just mean engaging in risk taking behavior, they mean disbelieving that ANY BEHAVIOR IS RISKY.

Do you understand the difference? I am beginning to. With that comprehension there is also an awareness that I do not leap out of bed each morning because I am eager to begin another day of love – I sort of crawl out of bed each morning.

We have nothing to fear. That is truth. This life is chosen. We are eternal beings of light here to manifest a physical reality that demonstrates love in the third dimension. In order to do that we need to absorb any thought that does not begin with love.

Every thought springs from you and YOU ARE LOVE. We are one force and we have been ignoring the power in that. We are love actualized. **The truth in the love that you are has been hidden beneath generations of fearful living.**

Our minds are open now, we can hear the truth and it is not unimportant. It is vital. **Love yourself and in that one action you will transform life on earth.**

Opposition can only exist if we are separate. WE ARE ONE. There is nothing to fear, nothing to fight, nothing to fix. When those thoughts of fear, fight or fix emerge, love them and tell them that that is not what you are doing any longer. It is ok, they are ok, yet you have realized the truth. Your life begins and ends with love.

The answer to any question must come from love. I have so very much more to say, yet this quest has come to completion for now. There will be another.

In these days ahead, remember that fear is an illusion; the power is in your hands. Love yourself and visualize the life and the world you want. Visualize love. Unity. Peace.

Do not accept any other picture of this world. The world is what we are creating, right now, with every thought. Choose your thoughts; do not think them as a reaction to what you see, but rather as a statement of what you KNOW.

It does not matter what anyone else is telling you, the power to change is within and it comes from you. There is no one else who controls your life. You do. You are so very beautiful and powerful and beneficial. You are key to this shift. Your love is paramount. Your gifts are vital and we are all depending on you to show us the way.

Fear is not real, but YOU are. Thank you for coming now and sharing this amazing time with me, with us. I love you absolutely.

*Blasts from the Past

Prelude

Here is the invite from the Face Book event held in November of 2011:

"This is a Quest for Love. In the seven days it lasts, you will be asked to notice it and then do something about the noticing. There is nothing else that feels like love; it is everywhere, and it does not need a reason.

This love that we are looking for is what will shift not only your life, but mine. It is what this whole "end of time" thing is about. It is not the end of you or this planet, it is the end of polarity.

This shift is not something we are waiting for. It is something we are doing. We are doing it now.

Please join us as we explore the idea of no boundaries, no separators, no differences. Just love. There is a gradual un-learning that has to occur before the re-learning of oneness settles in. It is an unraveling that may be disturbing and challenging because things are not as they once were.

You and I are the force beneath this shift of the ages. Together we have been afraid and judgmental and alone. The time for that is over. The time for unity is upon us now.

Love does not need a reason. The truth is that there is no reason to hold back, not any more. The old rules no longer apply. It is time to accept who you are without fear of any kind. You are divine perfection, a piece of the One Source. It is love for no reason that will change your life, your vibration and this world. We are ONE. Once you love YOU, knowing yourself completely, you will love everyone without condition. We are all waiting. See you on the Quest."

Day 1

It is 11.1.11, a day of symmetry.

This was shared on my personal Face Book page...

"I am hoping to share thoughts on this quest in a more active way. My thoughts are recorded here to stimulate additional ideas. If you feel inspired, comment directly on the Face Book event page for the love quest, so that we all can benefit. This simple act may go a long way to promote unity with us... we have all come to this quest for different reasons and yet we are one. Let's act like it."

Some additional comments concerning the "Occupy Wall Street" movement...

"The 99% movement is an expression of the shift... yet in it, there exists polarity. The families who make up the 1% are also part of the ONE that we are. On some level we know this, and the solution will come when all are served equally."

Day 5

"The OWS (Occupy Wall Street) movement is a historical moment, a demonstration of a unified field of awareness.

We have changed within and thus have added energetically to the possibility of it at all. It feels so very important that we notice what is happening. We are changing, we are letting go of fear, and we are coming out of our homes, removing our chains of fear and shifting in consciousness as an entire race and we are doing so from our living rooms. This is really happening. It is here. The time is right now and you are a vital component."

Day 6

"I have been thinking more about the Occupy Movement. It feels so very powerful. It feels like revolution, not in the sense of revolting against something, but as in joining with something. The power in that is palpable.

There is no leader. There is no violence. It is just Unity. This is unheard of for the planet, for the species. AS ONE we are speaking. AS ONE we are occupying. AS ONE we are changing the world."

Judgment

Prelude*

> Welcome to the Love Quest.

> It will last for one week.

> Each day for 7 days, upon waking, look into your own mirror and deeply into your own eyes.

> Say "Hello there."

> Say "I love you."

> Say "You are perfect, *right now.*"

> Smile. Let yourself feel that unconditional love for a moment.

> Now begin your day.

Welcome. Please follow along one day at a time.

This is not a race. Everyone wins on the Love Quest.

Day 1*

Hello and welcome to our Quest for Love.

While on our journey, I stop for several moments each day, and reflect on "why am I here?" and "what am I doing?" and "is this serving me?"

It is always about love and fear. It is always crystal clear, until it isn't. Today, for me, it isn't. The clarity has become muddled. Life has become flooded with energetic shifts that seem to be blowing me all over the place. I am stronger than ever and yet, more sensitive as well. It is an interesting perspective, to feel more certain and at the same time, perplexed.

The entire world is in a flux. There are names of groups and people who are to blame and at the same time who are going to swoop down and save us. It is the greatest time to be alive and really, without leaving my laptop, the greatest show on earth.

Yet regardless of what is going on outside of me, it will always come back to me. What determines every moment is my perspective. Quantum physics tells us this. We affect the events in our lives - Every single one of them. As I think about this, well, it gives me pause. I hope it does for you as well. *"Every single one of them."* Nothing is static, solid or pre-determined.

The only one I can count on is me. I determine what my life becomes. I have two possibilities here, both equally available. One is love, and the other is fear. They are called many names. The "reality" swirling around me will be seen out of my loving eyes or my fearful eyes, and that will make all the difference. I will make all the difference.

The most singularly powerful thing we can do to affect this life positively, is to love ourselves. **Self-love, as the lens with which we view all others, heals**. Self-abuse does not. We cannot hate ourselves and be a help to anyone else, or truly love anyone else.

The shift in consciousness starts in your heart. The truth of you is that you are love and you always have been. To realize that, in this very dense third dimension, is the challenge before all of us. To see each component of the "you" that lives here now, reading these words, and love anyway, wow. That is mastery.

Thank you for joining our Quest. See you tomorrow.

Day 2*

It is our second day.

As I write this I am close to tears, and not in a bad way. I am humbled and honored to be in the presence of so many teachers.

I realize once again that the love I am looking for, the answers I seek, have been right in front of me. They exist in every moment; in my children, my siblings, my friends, my parents, all by prior arrangement. The arrangements were mutual. There is never just one lesson, or one benefactor. I do not know the intricacies of each one, yet I trust the assistance gained was universal.

On this journey to agape I crashed into myself. I found a part of me I despised. Once discovered, I saw her everywhere. She was most obviously reflected in my closest relationships. There was no one else good enough, who loved me enough, who acted the right way or gave me enough of what I wanted to be happy. I was miserable. There was no consoling me and no happiness.

Oh, I looked ok. I smiled and exchanged pleasantries. I did the jobs I was asked to do. Yet, there was a part of my heart that was not engaged. It was shut down. Those that know me best knew this. They left me alone for a bit. I did not know what happened. This was a version of myself I had not seen in many years.

The point here is that first of all, I still don't know what happened but it doesn't matter. Secondly, I am better now, thanks in no small part to some very surprising people. ***You never know where an angel is lurking.***

Love is everywhere. It exists in every particle of life in this dream. There is never NO LOVE. There is only a time when you have put a lid on it. You may be wearing blinders, but it is out there. You may have yourself covered in plates of armor so you cannot feel it, but there is always that smile, or hug, or sunset, or laugh that will break through your armor and reach you.

You see we are connected. It does not matter who you are, or who I am. I cannot see you now but I know you love me. I don't know your age or your sex or your color or your country or your god, but I know who you are. You are love. You are divine. You are me and we are ONE.

I am so grateful to be part of this trip. The rise up to love, the realization of unity, the discovery of our holiness; all happening right now – it is happening to you, to me, to all of us.

I have been intensely on this journey for 12+years, and not so intensely for my entire life. I thought I understood. I did not. I thought, even now, that there was some love that was "better" than others, and that I was meant to be with some more than others. I thought that there were degrees of love.

There are not. Love is love, and we are one. It is universal and it is complete and whole and it is you and it is me and it does not matter if we ever meet. We are the same stuff. I read about nationalities and star nations and generations and sexes, yet truly, it is all just costuming.

Yes, there can be different degrees of comfort but truly, once you see without the lens of judgment you will see only love.

Those that are the least lovable are our greatest teachers and our brightest lights.

Thank you for sharing this journey...I love you absolutely.

Day 3*

Welcome to your third day on this Quest for Love.

There is nothing more important than self-love. It is the basic ingredient for a powerful authentic life. Lack of judgment is key. We have to give up any attachment to outcome or condition. Love is paramount. It must be the starting point of any situation. Love always yields the most fruit.

In order to be free, we have to give up our attachment to being "right". There is immediate pleasure in being right, believe me, I know. Yet it is temporary. "Rightness" and "Wrongness" are conditional; love is not. Love exists outside of behavior, regardless of attitude and in spite of age, race, social status, health or religion.

Love brings pleasure under any condition – it is a validation, and an authentic one, of YOU. YOU are LOVE. This is truth.

In this life now, I am a woman, a teacher, a writer, a mother, a daughter, and a sister. Yet all of these roles do not define who I am. Who I actually am, is love.

Here is the thing. I have to love in any situation. I have to stand in non-judgment. Once I do, the answer to every question will be the same; and it will be love.

You are here as an expression of the truth, a physical manifestation of love.

So, love yourself. Love your hair, your thighs, your feet, your eyes. Love the way you laugh, the way you sing, the way you show up every time. Love yourself in the morning, in the bathroom, on the bus and in the kitchen. Love the way you talk to your boss, pay your bills, shop for groceries, sit in class and stand in line. Love how you put on your shoes. Love and accept every thought you have, knowing that it will give you more thoughts with which to construct your amazing life.

Perfection cannot be defined. It is you. It is me. It is every single one of us. There are not enough cameras to photograph perfection. Think about beauty (as depicted in classical art) and how over time it has morphed from what we would call obesity to near anorexia (in women). Beauty is subjective.

Facts do not exist, (except perhaps in Math, yet even there you will find subjectivity). The things I learned in science and English and geography are no longer true. Pluto is not a planet, "ain't" is in the dictionary, and some of the countries I memorized, in order to illustrate my intelligence and to pass exams in school, no longer exist.

I am here, you are too and we stand or sit on earth most of the time. The rest is subjective. We are not here to judge ourselves according to anything that we see with our eyes. We are not here to judge. We are here to love.

Start with you. Love yourself today. The love felt within will emanate outwards. It is a force 5,000 times more powerful than any other thought your brain can come up with.

Just love. Every inch of you is perfection. Our brain cannot fathom the power in that love. Our hearts know. You have felt love and you have seen love. Now it is time to embrace love as the most vital component of your life.

Love is not to be thought about occasionally, love is to be felt continuously. If you are in doubt, just love. Your life will transform.

Thank you for sharing this Quest with me.

Day 4

We are half way there.

I have spent awhile now seeing life without the blinders of fear and it is glorious. To live fearlessly is magnificent. It has nothing to do with daredevil stunts or wealth beyond measure. It has to do with showing up - *Every time*, with looking at life, ALL OF LIFE, and seeing the inherent beauty it holds. There is an exquisite pleasure in connecting to another soul. It does not matter if you know this person, if you will ever see them again, if they are your waiter, your client, your sister, or the cashier. The connection is why we are here.

Life in this third dimension is intensely physical. It smells, tastes, sounds and feels constantly stimulating. This is why we come. This is why you will hear so many refer to us as the "masters". We are in a constant barrage of information and while doing so, we are remembering the truth of ourselves.

This is quite a feat, and it is not for the faint of heart. Give yourself a pat on the back. Since you are on the Quest, you know. You realize how critical it is to forgive yourself, to accept how you have shown up, and to love yourself. It is the start of everything, the beginning and the end, the alpha and the omega. You are the greatest show on earth, a most powerful being, here to remember all of what you are.

In order to move forward, we must leave judgment behind. Judgment is the root cause of so much unhappiness. Judgment takes work. We must constantly access and rate each moment, each person, each outcome and then decide if it pleases us or not, if it is acceptable or not, if it is good or bad, if we approve.

It is time to give that up. Let it go. It takes too much time and it does not matter. In truth, this is a dream and none of what we are looking at is real. The only thing that is real is love. Love is what you are, and what I am.

I may make mistakes, I may be horribly inappropriate, I may smell, I may shout at you, I may hurt you; but all of that will change and I will always be love. In the next moment I may make you laugh, I may excite you, engage you, thrill you and help you. I may be the one you were waiting for, the one who reminds you that you too, are love. I may introduce you to a way of life you would have never seen without me. I may insult you, I may steal from you, I may abuse you, and I may fall in love with your spouse. I may be your daughter, your lover, your enemy, your mother. In fact, I am all of those things, and I've done all of this and more.

When you judge me, you are, in truth, judging yourself. Once you accept yourself, right now, as you are, with every mistake, fault, imperfection and weakness, you will no longer judge me. You will see yourself as me; you will see me as yourself.

A highly evolved love of mine once shared a story with me. It went like this. He was up late with a dear, close friend who was struggling and talking, and talking and talking and as the night moved into the early morning an interesting thing happened... his friend *became* him. He was seeing himself, hearing himself, talking to and comforting, himself. In real time, with his human eyes, he was looking at himself; an astounding validation of what this life really is.

You are I are the same. Thank you for showing up and reminding me of this.

I love you.

Day 5

Welcome to the other side. We are more than half way through this Quest. We've had lots of opportunities to contemplate love.

Forgive me if I repeat myself, but it bears repeating — Non-judgment makes solid ground. With sure footing all of life is equally appreciated.

Judgment takes effort, enormous amounts of it. In order to be ready to judge, you must be constantly on guard, at the ready with an opinion and a label.

It is time now to put down these tools of discrimination — we are ONE. You are a nanosecond in eternity, one expression of the whole and regardless of your opinion about it, you will continue. *Just how your experience feels, is up to you.*

Decide to love your life. Be happy for no reason. There are many times in my day when I question my choices, if not my sanity. "Why did I pick this job?" "What is going on with my hair?" "What was I thinking when I said I would do this?" Depending on my frame of mind, these thoughts could escalate into depression or fun. Choose fun.

This is a dream, a game we have decided to play and sometimes, well, it stinks. Other times, it is mind-blowing and orgasmic. But either way, it's mine. It is what I have made. It is what you have made; a wondrous expression of life, created with all the awareness, talent and equipment we both had at the time.

You stand without requirement. You need nothing in order to be. You ARE.

YOU ARE LOVE. There is really nothing else to say. Words fail me when I notice the wonder of life, of you, of us. Our language does not provide enough of them.

It is your goal to love yourself, to see yourself, as Source beholds you. **There has never been one such as you and there will never be again. You are unique. This moment, with your contribution to it, is perfection.** *You stand without requirement.*

Acceptance is the beginning of self-love. Accept where you are now. I have decided that it is ok that I will never be as organized as some, as fit as some, as rich as some, as beautiful as some... I am. I came this way so that I could be. I did it. I am. All that I have to do now is pay attention. When I do, every moment brings wonders.

When I connect with everyone I meet in my day, I have the validation I seek. In each other's eyes, I see the love that we are. Look at your mail carrier, the cashier, your spouse, your child, your mom, your boss, your neighbor, the person standing behind you in line, the person sitting next to you on the bus or on the train, your client. Meet their gaze. You will see the light that you are, gaze back at you and I guarantee it will fill you up. It is the gift we are here to give to each other. It is why we gather, why we seek each other out.

We have grown fearful and we sit alone in coffee shops, move away from each other in elevators, and stare straight ahead while standing in line. Watch the children; they are looking at everyone, talking to everyone, taking us all in and the vitality shines from their very pores. This is what the shift will do for us as well. The eternal fountain of youth is love. It is us, it is free and it is here.

It only takes a time or two and the fear dissipates. Not everyone will meet your gaze, but when they do, the reward will keep you going. The prize is love and the supply is endless. There are no winners or losers, we all get some. That is how it works. This is the shift to love.

Thank you for being here,

Day 6

Hello everyone, and welcome to our sixth day. I would like to focus on something very specific today. I do not believe it will take a very long time to introduce, but don't be fooled, it will take some time to assimilate. The idea of self-love is quite radical, actually.

We have all heard about the importance of self-esteem, and to "love your neighbor as yourself". Yet while that song was playing in one of our ears, in the other ear we were hearing society tell us not only "where" we "should" be standing, but "how" we should be "acting" while we were standing there. These "shoulds" varied according to your age, sex, gender, social status, nationality, religion or occupation. Much pressure has been placed on your mere existence.

You stand without requirements. Loving yourself, as you are right now, is the most critical point in this entire evolution. You, in truth, have no requirements. You are perfect as you stand, how you stand, and where you are standing. This is the absolute truth.

Once you love yourself absolutely and accept yourself completely, you will stop looking outside of yourself for validation. You will not need a certain income, a specific car, a perfect weight or job or lover or outfit. Trophies and prizes will not be necessary. It won't matter if people tell you how wonderful you are, or if you feel as if you are appreciated or understood. You will stand without requirement.

The shift to self-love will dramatically alter all of your relationships. You will show up needing nothing from them. You will merely be, and what you will be - is love. You will show up as love, for that is the absolute truth of you.

You will be fearless, for nothing that anyone can do, will change the love you feel for yourself. Nothing can damage the love that you are.

You are complete and whole and perfect. I love you without condition and it is an honor to join you on this shift to agape.

Day 7

We made it. We have travelled together on this Quest for Love and have arrived.

Yet, where are we?

We are standing right where we began, sure footed and strong. Our light is streaming forth ever stronger now. As we can see clearly where we are; we are seeing *ourselves*.

This is scarier than any outside "enemy". We have succeeded without weapons or armies. We have done so alone. At these final moments of the journey, we are seeing how we never needed an army. All that we needed is within. We possess any imagined "requirement" to succeed. In truth, we always have.

The love that you are is available to you in your darkest, most lonely and frightening hour. It can be ignited by anyone, by any word, thought or vision. There is no "right" or "only" way to find love and truth. It is not necessary that you be in a place of worship or in service to a greater purpose than yourself.

There is no greater gift, no higher purpose, than to love. To realize love, and to create from that realization is why you are here.

You are simply, purely, and absolutely – love. You were created as perfect as perfect could be. It is ok to see yourself as flawless. You are. You do not have to brag or boast or shout or convince others of your greatness. Just be. They will know.

Think about the lion – a glorious beast who has never told anyone it was magnificent. When you gaze upon a lion, you know of its splendor and its power. A lion knows its own majesty, without a doubt.

It is time you knew of yours. Once you know, once you realize the love that you are, words will not be necessary. You will no longer need outside validation. You will live, as love, without requirements.

This is who you are.

It is an honor to have travelled with you. See you on the next Quest.

I love you.

*Blasts from the past

Prelude

Here is the invite that was sent. It was December of 2011.

This is a Quest for Love. Self-Love. It starts with you and ends with me and organically becomes US. We are one.

As this journey progresses, we will explore self-love. Self-love is the answer to every question. You and I are one. As I understand and accept every facet of who I am, I cannot help but extend that understanding and acceptance out to you...and we have unity. Oneness.

The Shift of the Ages is the shift in consciousness from polarity to unity. This shift is internal and simultaneously being expressed externally...the OWS (Occupy Wall Street) movement is an example of that expression, but if we are paying attention, it is evidenced everywhere.

Each day of this quest I will explore, in a message sent to your inbox, Love. You are invited to share on this page your own experiences of love, and success is not necessary here... we are growing, evolving as one. It is a journey; all moments are necessary steps forward. There are no mistakes.

This Quest is never ending...it is merely evolving.

Here is a Rumi Quote that depicts where we are heading...into a world with no edges.

"The clear bead at the center changes everything. There are no edges to my loving now.

You've heard it said there's a window that opens from one mind to another. But if there's no wall, there's no need for fitting the window or the latch."

It is my understanding that agape, complete self-love, creates for each of us that "clear bead at the center" to which Rumi refers. A worthy goal.

Day 1

"I am speaking to myself. I am struggling this morning. There is some blame, there has been anger. I can name many outside influences as reasons but truthfully, it always comes back to me. There is nothing else that is true. I can be as mad as I please (and believe me, I was), but this argument is all mine. I am mad at myself. Wow. That is a pill I do not want to swallow.

What I want to say today, as we begin this Quest and I am pretty crabby ;), is that I can't blame my sour mood on outside energy or the date or the banks or my lover or the galactic federation (smile). I am crabby because I don't love myself.

This is a realization that is perfectly timed. We are on a Quest to unconditionally love ourselves. It is time to notice those conditions in which I don't. There are apparently boatloads."

Day 2

"I find myself having learned a great deal these past 24+ hours... It has been very, very busy, all about family, and all about love."

Day 3

"Today has been hailed as a critical date – 12.12.11. There is talk of ascending and of huge waves of energy flooding this planet. I can only speak to what I am sure of, to what I "know", and I am sure that an emotional shift to love will positively impact your life as well as mine. I know that a focus on love will help all of us.

I hear Deepak Chopra speak of inner turbulence and I say "yes". That is the explanation for what I am compelled to speak of, to make video's about, to write about; calming our inner turbulence, and loving ourselves. This is what will shift this planet."

"I recently responded with fear. I had some unexpected news regarding my financial security and I immediately spiraled downhill. I became afraid and once I did, everything was colored differently. The world became a bit more frightening. Once I crossed into fear, I had to recognize it and climb back out. This Quest has supplied the ladder, and I am just about there.

My ego self-loved my fearful attitude, for I was very much OF THIS WORLD. I "forgot" who I was, and I felt threatened.

How can you threaten love? It is the basis of life."

Relationship

Prelude

> Welcome to the Love Quest.
>
> Each day for 7 days take a moment to look at yourself in the mirror.
>
> Look into your own eyes.
>
> Smile with your eyes and your mouth.
>
> Rest there for a moment.
>
> Say "Hello there. Today we are going to be with each other all day."
>
> Say "I love you. I honor our relationship. I can't wait to see where you take me."

Welcome. Please follow along one day at a time.

This is not a race. Everyone wins on the Love Quest.

Day 1*

Hello. I hope this finds you in a good place.

What do you believe about today? What do you believe about each relationship, project, love and person you are dealing with right now? That is what you will have. *You will have whatever you believe in.* You will SEE whatever you believe is there.

What is true is that it is all love. This dream is love expressed; YOU are an individual expression of that love. So am I. So is your neighbor, your friend and that guy who drives you nuts.

The thing is, love is the unifying field on which we are all playing. Each act/relationship makes use of individual actors, makeup, costumes and scenery. The layers and multitudes don't matter, beneath them all it's the same. There is a beginning, middle and end, every time.

Once complete, with makeup and costumes off, behind the actors and set; what is left is a mirror. You have been watching yourself all along. YOU have been feeling every nuance and living every moment, experiencing yourself. That is why you are here.

You are here, to experience yourself. In order to do that, you relate to me, to your family, to your neighbors, to your friends, to your lovers. In these relationships, you will feel every possibility;

pain, pleasure, fear, sadness, joy, fun, challenge, hope. Sometimes it is you who will initiate the dialogue/event, sometimes it is the "other" who starts things up. It doesn't matter where or how it begins, what matters is how you experience it. You will define what it means, for YOU. This life is YOU, experiencing yourself.

I am in an interesting place with this. I know these truths and yet, well, I am looking at a whole bunch of people as if they are to blame for initiating my discomfort. I KNOW THIS IS NOT TRUE, and yet, with each interaction, I find myself thinking they are at fault. I have not been here for quite some time. The timing of this is interesting.

I believe that I am re-visiting all of my negative patterns just now so that I can make a choice. The choice being – will I walk this belief (or is it just talk)? I cannot even take myself seriously with all of this. My internal dialogue is feasting on my confusion – "why did I say that?" "what are you doing?" "who do you think you are?" ... My old egoic self is ecstatic. It is looking like she is going to be returned to the throne after all.

She has forgotten my tenacity, and my insatiable desire to be happy. This is why I came just now. At this time in our collective history it is possible to experience joy in our every moment. Once we know and can actualize the secret, we are free to love without condition.

The secret is simple. Love yourself. We are the same. The divinity that runs through me also swims in your veins and courses through every component of life. We are ONE and as such there is nothing ever that is done TO YOU. Everything is created BY YOU.

On this Quest we will explore our illusions of good and bad and right and wrong love. For today, let's just sit with the thought that WE are love. Our realization and acceptance of that truth is the source of our power.

I love you. Thank you for showing up.

Day 2

Welcome to the second day of this journey.

Today I'd like to explore the idea of being hurt. It is a thought we all hold about someone, somewhere, at some point in time. We believe that they were/are responsible for our own pain.

I have my own list. it includes entire groups of people as well as numerous individuals. I have spent many hours sharing my painful stories and they are convincing. If you read them now, no doubt you'd agree, much to my satisfaction.

As I walk this journey to agape, I see that I have to let go of any blame. I can't walk around saying "I love you", while, at the same time and pointing in another direction, saying "But I don't love you".

First of all, it feels really bad to say those things and I mean on an energetic level.

Try it. Think and feel the words "I love you" and notice the happiness, even if it's not full out. Somewhere there is the internal hope that it could be true (loving YOU), and that feels good.

Now think about someone who in your mind fits the description "But I will *never* love <u>you</u>". As you think and say and feel those words, notice the heat, the anger, the discomfort and displeasure you experience.

No one else is there. You have experienced the positive and the negative all on your own. You did this. He or she was not even aware of your conversation, they cannot be responsible. The negative emotion began and ended with you. You are talking to yourself.

Now, which feels better? It's all a choice. You are in complete control of how you feel. That will always be true.

Things happen and not all of them are fun. In fact, up until now many of them have been downright awful. You cannot hide from these things. They have been a part of this life you are living. What you can do, from a new perspective, is decide to live the best life you can, regardless of them. You can decide to love anyway.

Your power comes from that decision. Blame puts the responsibility for your life in the hands of someone else, someone who is not you. The only one responsible for your happiness is you. The only one who can love you without any opinion at all —

is you. Loving yourself is paramount. It is not selfish or foolish. It is empowering.

Decide to be happy. Decide to feel good about who you are. For today, for now, for this journey; just focus on loving, caring, understanding and accepting YOU.

This is not done in spite of all the "unlovable" that is out there — for that idea carries with it a thought that does not start with love.

This is done with a focus on love.

If there is ever to be a shift in our collective hearts, it has to begin here, in your single heart. We operate as one and each thread in this fabric of creation is woven together perfectly for maximum strength and beauty.

It all matters. Every thought that runs through you can support you. Notice what depletes you and on faith alone, let it go.

Love supports you. Every time. You, who have lived through all that has happened, are love. You are perfect. **You have been waiting for someone to believe in;** *you are here.*

I believe in you. I know who you are. You are love, you are me, we are one and we can do this.

Day 3

Welcome to the third day. How are you feeling? The idea is to feel empowered. This is your Quest. You are in search of the love of your life. You are looking for that wonderful feeling of recognition and adoration. What we are out to discover is the location of agape – unconditional self-love.

We have looked at love as something we "fall into", something we are given (if we are lucky) from someone we have given it to. We have defined it, denied, it, ignored it and regretted feeling it. Mostly, we have misunderstood it.

Love exists as the core substance of you.

You were lovingly breathed into life and sit here now as a physical body experiencing whatever you choose. It does not matter what your age or sexual orientation is, where you live or if you practice a religion; your essence is love. Love is what sources your existence.

Love is a fact of life. It is truth. It cannot be destroyed. Love and relationship are not the same things. Much of our discomfort with love surrounds intimate relationships. We've had "good" ones and "bad" ones, and been left feeling, perhaps, that we didn't really understand love, or that love hurts, or that we'll always be lonely or that we must be unlovable. None of these things hold up in the face of this truth – *love is what you are.*

Whom you choose to share yourself with in a tangible way will shape your experience of love, but it will not change love. Love is. If you have felt it for one – they have felt it for you in return. Period. That fact doesn't guarantee a relationship of any kind, but it is truth.

You've seen another, made eye contact and *felt them.* That feeling now running through you is love – it is the connection point, recognition. You may look away, run away or start a conversation; the choice is yours. This is the beginning of relationship. That relationship can go many ways. You may start a business together, find out you have nothing in common, become lovers, friends or enemies. None of those things you do with the connection changes the love. The love exists. It may not manifest into anything that you deem worthy or "good", in fact, it may feel really "bad", but it does not go away.

These descriptions of the relationships begun and experienced around love do not erase or alter the love that was mutually felt. You cannot change the love, whether or not you have the relationship you believed you wanted.

We are all at choice. We can see love and choose to explore it or not, enjoy it or not. What we cannot choose to do is eliminate it.

It is never true that love is a waste of time; or that you are unlovable or unloved. Look around and recognize the feeling when you meet another's eyes to whom you are connected. You shine a little brighter, are lifted a bit and feel better for the moment. This person may be your child, your grandmother, your lover or the cashier at the market — yet the love was mutually felt and understood.

That's what love does, it lifts you up. It is like a reminder of truth.

Never give up on love. If your lover, child, friend or relative disappoints you it does not mean they have stopped loving you. It means they have stopped acting in a way that pleases you. They get to.

WE ARE FREE. The hallmark definition of love is freedom. Love in physical form can create comfort, yes, but that comfort will never come from control. Those you love are free to express themselves in an infinite variety of ways, as are you. Loving another does not mean controlling their behavior or whereabouts. Love does not mean restriction in any sense.

Love means freedom. Relationships change yet love does not. Your most intimate relationship is the one you have with yourself. Care for it and recognize it as the basis of all of your other relationships. Love yourself without condition. Once you do, you will recognize the love in all of your relationships – "good" or "bad", current or not.

You are a divine spark of love and sometimes you meet another one and erupt into a magnificent fire – other times, regardless of how many attempts, there is barely a flame. The conditions weren't right or other choices were made. This does not mean that the conditions can't change, they may. Another day or another lifetime and that connection can be re-kindled to create anew.

It's all choice, yours and theirs. It's all love, eternally love. You don't have to wait to find yourself any longer. Just notice the love that you are and once you peek out from behind your dark glasses, you will feast on your own magnificence. You will see love everywhere you look because YOU are reflected in everything you see and YOU ARE LOVE.

I can see you already.

You are brilliant.

Thank you for sharing your Quest with me.

Day 4

You are midpoint on this Quest.

The truth about love – that it is everywhere, that we can access it without anyone else in the room – is a challenge. This way of thought is not one we are familiar with.

I hope you'll stay with me here as I have some ideas to offer you that are not what we've been fed all along. The reason I offer them on this Quest is so that ultimately, we can adopt a strategy for living and loving that *lasts*. Not just for a moment or a weekend or a few short months – forever.

I want us to feel always empowered, always loved, and always love. My deepest wish for us is constant joy. This is not dispensed to us from an all-powerful source, but *it springs from us*.

It's like tying your shoes. Having tied shoes is something you took for granted as a toddler. Every day, some adult in charge, tied your shoes. If they became untied and loose, you could trip and fall. Although you may have been able to get back up again, you could not prevent another fall because you were not able to tie your own shoes.

Until you learned. It wasn't easy. It felt clumsy and often they came undone anyway. Daily, sometimes hourly practice changed all that. One day they didn't get loose and you didn't trip at all. A few days later you stopped thinking about your shoes. You just skipped through your days, unafraid.

We all have different approaches. One of my sons just ties them once. Not once a day, or once a week, but once – period. He hates tying his shoes and enjoys the freedom of never thinking about it beyond that moment when he brings them home from the store. It works.

So, let's skip through our days, unafraid. Let's lose our dependence on some "other" to love us and create a feeling of worth in ourselves. Let's access our very essence and love ourselves. That way, no matter whom else is around, we are ok. We can feel good, joyful even. We can take pleasure in the wonder of us, in the fact that we breathe and think and communicate and create. Let's enjoy ourselves without dependence on another to create that possibility.

Happiness, joy, love – it's all a choice. It is not something we have to ask for. It is the expression of our very nature. We are powerful, playful, loving beings. We are here now, by choice, to "shift the vibe" from polarity to unity. This really is who you are;

you are a unique form of creative energy who came to do this wonderful thing. You are here to love.

Your understanding and willingness for the role is breathtaking. You are seeking to learn. You are looking to evolve. Your unique gift is necessary. We all need who you are.

You stand without need of improvement. You require nothing else to be of value. You are beautiful, strong, compassionate and perfect. You can hear these words again and again or never again – they are truth.

Speak them to yourself. When you fall, get up and lovingly tie your own shoes and join us as we skip through life with our own shoes firmly tied. We are smiling and strong and waiting for you.

We know who you are without words. When our eyes meet, you tell us.

You are love.

Day 5

Hello. Let's get right to it.

Love is divine. The divinity spoken of is not reserved for the love of a god or a child, but for all expressions. Understand that once love is recognized, there are an infinite number of ways for it to be felt and shared. There are connections that are spiritual, some that are mental, those that are emotional and others that are physical. All are love.

We have put labels on love; defined love as "good" or "bad", real or otherwise. In truth, love exists in all moments. It is the recognition of that love in each facet of life that propels us towards unity.

Labels are separators, and as long as they exist, oneness does not. All is love. That wild sexual encounter, quiet walk in the park, gentle hug, inspired dance, passionate conversation, angry outburst and helping hand are each physical manifestations of love; each very different, yes, but with the same "value".

Love cannot be quantified, I do not love one of my children more than the other. I love each of my children. I do not love one of my siblings more than the other. I love my siblings. It is the same with each of my friends, all of my bosses, and every one of you. I love you all the same.

Love is like air. It surrounds us. We breathe it in and out and expect it to always be there. You don't wake up each day hoping you'll get enough air. You wake up and breathe it in. It sustains you.

Love surrounds you. It is equally available. It does not increase its power if you are rich or beautiful or lucky or of a certain race or religion or age. Love is an equally potent force for all of us. Whether it manifests as hundreds of friends or just one, it is the same.

How much you are loved is not indicated by numbers of any sort. You are loved. Like the air, there is no place you can look and not see love.

The trick is to recognize it. It's like that saying, "If you want to hide something, put it in plain sight." Love is right in front of you, every moment of each day.

This does not mean you will enjoy each moment, vision or person equally. You do not have to open your arms and hug them all. You will laugh with some of us, yell at some of us, dance with some of us, disagree with some of us and make love with some of us. You will feel closer to some than others. These are specifics of relationships, not degrees of love.

Love is truth. It is you. It is me. It is us. You have come here now to actualize the love that you have always been. You are here to realize your very essence.

There is no better time than now to love. I have a lifetime of stories I have shared and re-lived up until now, that don't serve the love that I am. They serve only to separate. I have believed that in order to understand me, you had to hear all of my sadness. Like a badge, I wore them and spoke of each mistreatment dramatically and effectively. What they had in common was someone to blame. That someone was not me. I am putting my badges away and you know, I feel a whole lot better.

Unencumbered, I am free to love without condition. I am ok, not in spite of my past or because of what's happened, but just because. There is no room in my life now for blame. The past is not real, it cannot be touched. What I can touch and feel and see and experience is this cat by my side, this pen in my hand and the sun outside my window.

What I have is right now. I watch my beautiful son eat his leftover birthday cake for breakfast (a questionable family tradition), and hear his adorable brother laughing and count my many blessings.

This is the world I have created and it is perfect. It's a bit messy, sometimes it stinks, but always it is life; my expression of the love that I am and that's okay. Actually, it's magnificent.

Today, let go of your propensity to label people and to judge levels and kinds of love or life. Give up judgment altogether.

Your moment to love is here and no one is better equipped to love yourself than you. There's no room for judgment in one such as you. You are a being of light and source runs through every part of you. There is nothing left to do but love. It is what you are.

I love you.

Day 6

Welcome to our sixth day.

You have looked at love directly on your Quest — not romantically or possessively or exclusively — you have looked at what it is. Today, let's look at what it isn't.

Much of my life I have spent harboring the idea that:

A. If you comply with my wishes that is evidence of your love for me, and
B. If you don't, that means you don't care about me, because
C. If you love me, you will give me what I want.

Love is not compliance, or obedience or submission. Relationships are full of all three. There is a difference between doing something because you are afraid and doing something from love. It is difficult to illustrate the difference in our actions alone because it is not the actions that define the love. It is the feeling beneath them.

When love motivates my actions, they create a feeling of well-being for both of us. When I act because I'm afraid of loss if I don't, then maybe my loved one is satisfied, but he is not loved and I don't feel great. The difference is felt internally.

In the U.S., there are all sorts of "holidays" created, I think, by the greeting card industry. We have Mother's Day, Father's Day and Valentine's Day. Our family has come to label them "Hallmark Holidays". They are lovely, sentimental days to spend in communion with your dearest loves. They are also days in which you are required to perform, as indications of your love.

Now there is nothing wrong with giving gifts on specific days to each other, but whether you do or not does not indicate your level of dedication or depth of feeling. One of my sons has labeled Valentine's Day "Singles Awareness Day".

One morning in early February, after just giving birth, I was able to zip up my jeans. It was a big deal and I was thrilled. That afternoon, I received a bunch of flowers in the mail from my partner, with a card that read "Happy Jeans Day". It was perfect and I was deeply touched. He spoke from his heart and my heart heard him. I have no idea if I ever received a Valentine that year. It didn't matter. I had received a real love note.

What is always true is that love does not need a special day or a specific mode of expression. What actions are done or not done have more to do with what's going on in someone's head than what's going on in someone's heart.

If I say no when you ask me to do something, it does not mean I don't love you. It means I don't want to, and that's okay. Now because I love you I will do my best to satisfy you. I won't always agree with you or be able to perform or have the desire to give you what you want. Those conditions are facts of my life right now, not indicators of my love.

It is easy to misidentify the actions of someone you are in relationship with. What you will never misinterpret is your own heart. As we are one, you know what I am feeling. This doesn't mean you know what I am thinking – you don't.

We are one and we can feel each other. It is that feeling that connects us. What we do when that feeling shows up is determined by our age, gender and current relationship. We express ourselves in unique ways, speak many languages and grow up in different families.

How we look may be very different yet how we feel in love will always be the same – connected. As we move towards unity consciousness our intuitive-self increases in sensitivity. Listen to your truth. You've been telling it to yourself right along.

You know love when you feel it. The actions of another have only to do with them. Act from love. Trust your truth. Intend love without requirements and your life will demonstrate only that.

You are the one you are waiting for. It is nice to "see" you here.

I love you absolutely.

Day 7

You've reached the completion of your Quest for Love. This has been a different sort of Quest. You have journeyed into places unseen. You've opened the door to your deepest held beliefs about others. You've faced squarely your expectations and requirements in love. You've examined your judgments about what love "should" do and "must" look like in order to be true.

You've discovered that regardless of what it *looks* like, love is always true. Love is identified by what it *feels* like, not what it looks like. You are love and stand as its source. You've been searching for it everywhere but the one place it exists. It begins and remains in your own heart.

Love does not show up in your life when someone else says "I love you". Love is what you are. It exists because you do. To recognize it in this very dense third dimension, filled with contrast and polarity, can be a challenge.

Start with you. These beliefs, attitudes, expectations, requirements and judgments are ideas we hold about ourselves. It is time to let them go. They are firmly rooted in right, wrong, good and bad. There is none of that in love. It's all love. You are worthy, deserving and uniquely suited to love. You are the perfect expression of love in physical form.

Feel wondrous about yourself. Appreciate your own magnificence. There is no reason to wait to love you. The time is today. Love yourself now.

You don't need to look or act a certain way before you can love yourself. You don't need to do a certain thing in order to prove that you love yourself. Just love yourself. Without condition.

Once you accept who you are, the rest is easy. There is no one harder on yourself than you. Listen to the way you talk to yourself — would you speak those words aloud to someone else? I think not.

Accept yourself without condition and go one step further — celebrate yourself. Give yourself the gift of appreciation. You, who understand deeply every part of yourself, are divine. You have no imperfections. In a world of infinite possibilities, you are merely one of them.

You have your own way of looking, being, acting and speaking. They are uniquely yours. You always do what you believe is the best thing to do in every situation. It is.

How things turn out and are received by others has more to do with what the "others" believe about themselves than you. It always comes back to you.

Love who you are today without any reservation. You stand without requirements. *Right now – you are perfection. Right now – you are love.* It is ok to love yourself.

Be the shift. It starts with you. It begins within. Don't wait for your lover or family or friends or country to love you first. There are no standards to comply to. You have met and exceeded them all. It is time to believe your most cherished secret – that *you are good and that you are capable of achieving your wildest dreams and that you are loved.*

You are. There is no one more perfect than you. There is no one more deserving of love than you. You are loved beyond your greatest imaginings.

This shift takes place in our hearts. Love yourself without any hesitation at all. Begin, right now, to say "yes".

Just love yourself.

Thank you for sharing your journey with me.

*Blasts from the Past

Day 1

This Quest took place in January of 2012. Here's a note from that first day.

"I am filled with anticipation for this year, this Quest, and all of the associated changes that go with both. The rehearsals are over. We have arrived. Perhaps we haven't been rehearsing all along, perhaps; just maybe, we have been IN IT each time until now.

It feels that way. That is the gift of this dream, it feels so real. Every moment feels like the final show. We set it up this way, and today, this month, this year, this time for all of us, feels especially urgent. It is and it is not. What is always true is that we are at choice to make this moment whatever we believe it to be. "

Intimacy

Prelude

Welcome to the Love Quest.

Begin and continue each day of this Quest with fearless acceptance.

When you look into your eyes each morning, stay there until a sort of doubt enters, a bit of fear, a hint of "I don't know if I can swim that deeply."

Begin then to smile and offer gentle encouragement.

It is going to be okay. You are going to make it.

You are confronting intimacy. It is the fuel for your passion and the depths of your love.

Smile with your eyes.

Embrace with your love.

Say "Hello. I have been waiting to meet you."

Say "It is time to come out of your hiding place."

Say "I will keep you safe. I'll hold you with gentility. I will not hurt you."

Feel that.

Now, boldly go forth to embrace the day in front of you. Fill it with you.

Welcome. Please follow along one day at a time.

This is not a race. Everyone wins on the Love Quest.

Day 1*

It is the first day of your Quest for Love.

Put aside the shoulds and the jobs and the rules of your life. *Just feel.* You are out to love yourself absolutely. You are here now to love you. You come first. Your life springs from you.

When you make something, it matters what material you use. If the glue you are using isn't strong, your paper Valentine will fall apart. Your love begins with you. The love you are projecting onto others is as strong as the love you feel for you.

You have to love you. This is not just a nice idea, or something to do after you love everyone else. This is where you begin. You are everything you've intended to be, complete and whole. You don't need an upgrade, a do-over or a revision to be worthy. You are worthy right now. Nothing else is needed. You are complete. Love yourself.

This is the only you available. You cannot trade yourself in to find a more compatible version. **Get to know yourself and you will find a depth of familiarity that exists in no other place.** Your most important relationship is the one with the mirror.

Look at yourself, unafraid. You are beautiful. There is none other who has walked in your shoes – you have done it all.

This you who is standing there chose to be here. This you who stands here is worth knowing. Resolve to know yourself. This journey to love yields many surprises. You may discover parts forgotten. Loving yourself for the first time is every bit as exciting as loving someone new. There are discoveries and there is unexpected joy. This is because "falling in love" with anyone is a projection of what you are feeling for you. There are others who show up and through them you get to remember how wonderful you are. It is so much fun.

When relationships end, at root cause is a lack of self-love. When someone new and thrilling becomes old and annoying it is not because they have changed. They may have, yet the "falling out of love" is not with them, it's with you.

No one can love you enough to make up for the lack of love you feel for yourself.

Loving yourself is mandatory.

You will face always choices and changes. With any decision there is a moment in which you must know who you are and what it is that you want. What *YOU* want, not what your mother or your lover or your society wants. *What you want.* This truth can only be discovered with fearless exploration. With eyes wide open and unafraid of judgment you must know yourself. If you don't, there will never be another who will do it for you. It is up to you.

Happy Quest Day.

Give yourself time to spend in fearless self-awareness. Do something just for you. Because, my love, you are worth it.

Day 2

This love of self is an interesting idea. It suggests that you value yourself, not more than anyone else, but as much. When I say "you come first", that is not the same sort of "first" as in a contest. Our language makes it difficult to speak of love in a way that conveys its truth.

"First" in a competitive sense suggests "better", at least for a specific moment in time. It could mean fastest, strongest, smartest or most beautiful. Our culture holds ideas of arrogance around considering yourself to be any of those things. This is because, I believe, we've been systematically beaten down. Competition is not our natural state, it was learned.

"You come first" because that is what life is.

Life is an exploration of self, of love; an evolving journey that you are undertaking, indeed that you are creating. You are the beginning, the starting point, and ultimately the focus point from which your life springs. Therefore, the statement "you come first" is merely truth.

What you feel and think about everything you are seeing, matters. It matters to *you.* Insight into those feelings and thoughts yields self-awareness. It becomes important in each interaction to know where you end and the other begins. Without that awareness, confusion reigns.

Relationships can be a mess. You care for someone and want them to be happy. You do something, perhaps believing that doing so will make them happy and yet they do not act happy, at least not for very long. Now you are confused and possibly hurt. "Don't you love me anymore?", "I did everything you wanted.", "I just don't know you anymore." This is the dialogue of a relationship in "trouble".

You cannot "make" anyone happy. You can be happy yourself and, in that happiness, I may experience joy. There is nothing you can do to alter what I feel about me. If I love myself, there will be spillover onto our relationship and you will witness my self-love. If I don't like myself, you will have a front row seat to my self-loathing. If we are intimately involved, I may even blame you for it.

You've been taught to do this. You believe there is fault and blame for both the "good" and the "bad" in your life. Both imply wrong. In a very real sense, with enough distance, you can step back and see that there is never "wrong". Each word and choice were the best you could come up with at the time and what I believed I needed to do in that moment.

This is why you must come first. If you understand what is at the core of these feelings, you are much more equipped to respond authentically.

You know authentic. It is not something you have to be taught. It has been labeled "conscience" and brings with it all sorts of confusing ideas around the "right" and "wrong" choices in love. Love is not right or wrong. Love exists. With your eyes open you will see it emanating from others with whom you relate. You know when it is there. It stands without being questioned, as no questions are needed – your whole being gives the answer and the answer is "yes".

This is the voice to trust. *This is the you that comes first.* This is who you must get to know, to honor and to fall in love with. He or she holds many wondrous truths for you, and about you.

You are multi-faceted, surprising, honest and true. You are the real thing. You are love and there are none greater than you. You are here now to contribute your voice to the symphony of love that we are as one. The music will not sound the same without you. All parts are required. For the purest, clearest contribution you must deeply comprehend your own voice.

The truth of you is right now whispering. Take a moment to listen, it is telling you which song to sing next.

Have an amazing day.

Day 3

There is much about love that is misunderstood, particularly love of self. This love of self has been labeled selfish, arrogant and demanding. You've been told it is wrong to put yourself first; so, in your mind, self-love brings guilt right along for the ride.

This is due to the "levels of importance" game that is played in the name of love. You have assessed how much love there is by looking at how much time is spent doing a specific thing. You have supposed there was such a thing as "more love" and its opposite, "less love". The evidence has been everywhere.

Attention, focus and length of time are not indicators of love; they are gauges of current interest level. We are multi-faceted, powerful, light filled beings of love; extremely capable of multi-tasking. Our brains are wired to differentiate. We've grown up in factory-type schools that graduate classes of identical products (instead of diverse human beings); all reaching for the same thing. The pull to uniformity and singularity runs deep in our psyche. It is not true to our nature.

As we awaken, and we are, we are opening our eyes to just how expanded we are – we can be good at more than one thing, enjoy many activities as well as many different people.

You can love more than one person and you can even love yourself.

Perhaps the most shameful and radical idea in all of this is the love of self. If you hear nothing else on this Quest, please hear this – **you are good enough to love**. The judgment about self-love is a falsehood. It is based on a misconstrued idea that was intended to create legions of people who feel really bad about themselves and who would then willingly follow any person or program which promised to change that.

Only you can change how you feel about you and it's okay – you are okay and in fact, **the possibility of you is beyond your wildest imaginings**.

You are made of the stuff that love is – the reason that sex is so fantastic is not because you are seeing God, it is because you are seeing *you – and you are that fantastic*.

The potential in you to do and focus on and love many, many things, activities and people is all rolled up into this physical manifestation of divinity called *you*. You are only at the beginning of discovery and many wonders await you.

You are just peeking through the door now. Soon it will be thrown wide open and the vision of you there will astonish you with love.

You are shooting for fantastic and the potential for that is right here, in you. Fall in love. Enjoy who you are. Your humor, your smile, your quirks, your abilities – all of that is the accumulation of intent – the intent of a Master.

You are that Master. You have come now to break out of these limits of self-loathing and appreciate the freedom that is love.

Love has no limits, and either do you. It is time to experience the freedom that is you.

Day 4

You are midpoint on your Quest.

Today I want to talk about love — not only love of self, but love of others. It happens with many fits and starts. It can be a mess.

So, what do you do? In order to be satisfied always, happy all the time and complete — what do you do? You listen to your heart. That is the easy answer.

You begin to trust that small voice that tells you truth. You allow it to speak, even in the face of potential disapproval. You will feel many different things in and around the notion of love — the feeling is not right or wrong, it merely exists. What you do about it, now this is where it becomes confusing.

Your relationship with someone does not define love, it defines that specific relationship. If we use different language to talk about our interactions and our feelings, maybe it will help to clarify things.

You can love anyone. You can be physically intimate with anyone who has reached sexual maturity. They are not the same thing. Except when they are, and here is the messy part. There is such confusion around love and lust, sex and romance that even the words can evoke judgment.

So, let's call it *love* for the feeling and *intimacy* for the act. Sex sounds like too loaded a word for our purposes. We are biologically and emotionally different. Our reasons for intimacy are as varied as we are. Our reasons for love are not.

Love is felt and understood universally. Love is encouraged and applauded. Love is depicted and discussed in every movie, play and song written. It is the driving force of your life here. **Love is who you are.**

You love all the time. Despite what the media and tabloids would have you believe, we aren't being intimate all the time.

We may mistakenly assume that any friendship where intimacy is possible (for physical reasons) always goes there. This idea keeps us fearful and shut down; removed from the very people you came here to engage with – us.

Does it actually work this way? Are you intimate with every man or woman with whom it is possible? Do you even want to be? Do you love these people? What is love anyway? Is it good or bad, right or wrong, healthy or unhealthy to love? What is keeping you from loving?

There is love. It is not up for judgment. It exists. You recognize it in the films you watch because *love is what you are.*

There are ways of expressing love – laughter, a smile, a listening, a helping hand, a tip, a cup of coffee, an intimate encounter, a reprimand, a loan, a promise. Each signifies the kind of relationship, not the amount of love.

You love others. There are some you take care of, some you laugh with, some you sleep with, some you marry. What you do with each other defines the relationship, not the love. All have merit; all are equal in value.

You've decided on a specific journey this time around and while on your path, you will meet many. There is no truth in judgment. It is only opinion and it is relative.

What I am trying to say here is judgment has no part in love. Love is, and only you know what form of expression it takes in any relationship that you are a part of. That knowing is the only truth to trust.

I witnessed a beautiful thing just last night. A dear love of mine has run straight into her deepest held beliefs about men and discovered that her lover has not been honest. She was not angry, she was introspective. It was an inner journey I watched as she examined how she truly felt about him, realized the gifts he had given her and that it was time to end it. It had run its course. Oh, she was hurt and it will be some time before she is ready to engage again, but truly, she was able to see what the relationship was, and what it wasn't. She listened to her heart.

Agreements and promises are not the same as love. If the agreement is monogamy, the love doesn't end when the monogamy ends, but the relationship probably does. Things run their course.

The only thing that has any chance at successfully getting you through this is your heart. It speaks quietly yet consistently. You know when you are doing the right thing. Not right in an "appropriate" sort of way; right for *YOU.*

This life will feel okay when the voice you are heeding is the one inside; it has only your best interests in mind.

No one else does. Not your lover or your mother or your friends — although they may want what's best for you and want you to be happy, they can't help but hold a skewed opinion about what would make that happen. They love you, yet they don't know you like you know you.

Self-awareness is necessary. Trust your own truth. *Your voice* is what should ring the loudest in your head. Once you decide to listen and move forward, you can be sure you are headed in the perfect direction for you; ***the voice in your head will become who you are.*** This is authentic power, and from that point you'll know always who you are. Your divinity was never in question.

Day 5

This love of you becomes the love of others not because it is the right thing to do in the context of religion or morality, but because *as you love yourself you are loving others. It is fact. You are the other.* Period. This is what is actually happening on our earth, with each of us as part of a collective.

As an organic whole, we have hated ourselves. In that hatred we have participated in universal self-destruction. The means of our deterioration have been warfare; chemical, monetary, psychological and physical control. We as a whole have been a part of it all. Our contribution individually has taken the form of self-loathing.

We are one. Every thought and feeling contributes to the whole. Each judgment and all of the negativity you held, and assumed didn't matter, because it was only self-directed – has contributed. You are an integral component of the whole that is us.

The systematic manipulation of us was part of the plan. You are here willingly participating in this life to challenge yourself. "What is it possible to create within so much negativity?" The odds of polarity have been stacked against you.

All that is changing now. You are changing that. You are beginning to love. Your light is peeking out from under its covering of darkness and I can see it. Our combined light is brightening this field on which we play.

There is no truth in a polarized life. You have never created alone. What you feel, you see, and all thoughts are creative. We are creating our life, our world, as one.

As we shift from self-hatred to self-love **the entire planet shifts.** Eventually, you will witness the effects of your love.

What can you do to change the world? You can love yourself, and your world will change.

It is not "just" you, it is *you.* You and your world become me and my world, which is us and our world; our world, our life, as one expression of love.

The individualized piece of divinity that you are, is every bit as important to what happens in this world as that piece that is a president.

This is not a falsehood. This is truth. *You are the starting point, the ending point, and the whole point.* **Love yourself.** *You will change the world.*

Day 6

Love is the beginning of everything. When you find you are experiencing a really intense negative feeling connected to a specific person, it doesn't mean there is something wrong with that person.

You feel so bad because you are not "in sync" with who you are and with what you came to do. That person is a mirror. You might even think of them as a gift. They are showing you something you've not noticed until now.

Love makes us feel so good because it is exactly what we are the very best at doing. You may be a great cook or hair stylist or carpenter or plumber or auto technician. These offer satisfaction and a sense of pride.

Loving fulfills you like nothing else can. It is your highest calling and the purest thing you can offer someone.

When I love myself without condition, I feel a sense of safe. With an absence of judgment, I experience freedom. Inside of unconditional love I can expand into my wildest imaginings of myself. I am free to be me.

Not the small version that worries about being accepted or liked or judged, but the grand version without limitation.

That kind of acceptance and love is what is waiting for you on the other side of polarity. When you give up good and bad, right and wrong – you become okay. Hang in there for a bit and you might just become terrific.

Once you see yourself as okay, the rest of your world, which is a reflection of you internally, becomes okay. It is this change that is shifting our time. See the world as okay and it will be.

When I came to accept myself, everyone else got a whole less annoying. (smile)

It was amazing.

You create your life. You are a creator, right now. You are the conductor of your piece, conducting it as you play it, reading the music you wrote yourself. It's all you. You are a virtuoso. There is no one with your command of this exquisite instrument that is you.

You are priceless, unique and perfectly crafted. Your song is an original. There are no wrong notes or words, only new verses that tell us where you are right now.

We all know the refrain – it reminds us of who you are – you are love. Whenever you get to that part, we all love to sing along. It's more fun that way and *YOU are our favorite melody.*

I love you every moment.

Day 7

We've completed our journey. We've gone some places and looked squarely at love. We've discovered that this journey, the one we are on from the moment we arrive, is really a hall of mirrors, like the ones you walk through at carnivals. At each turn you see you – yet very differently. At one point you appear much bigger than you thought and in the next moment, you look much smaller than everyone else. With each step there is another view and distortion, yet you know it's all ways and always you.

We love ourselves in everyone we see. They don't look like us yet they are reflections of how we feel about ourselves. We give them what it is we have. Our cup must be always full.

What empties your cup? When we began these Quests – we started with forgiveness. We started by looking in the mirror and saying "I forgive you". We did that for seven days. We've branched out and our journey has gone other places yet the destination is the same.

You are out to find self-love. What drains your cup is blame, it is fear and it is judgment. These are not tendencies that you were born with. These are learned. This Quest is about un-learning them.

You woke up today with everything you need to be worthy. You are here. I am so happy you have taken up this journey. Your smile, your whole essence contributes to the love you feel in these words and on this Quest.

This Quest was created by you. All of us are now basking in this love that you are.

You did this. You joined hearts with your own self-love and created an avalanche of love. Who knows how much love is gaining momentum each day that you love yourself just a little bit more?

I know it is a challenge to forgive yourself. After all, no one knows your mistakes like you do.

Look at the word 'mistake'.

Your life is like a show. You are eternal, yet for this moment now you've donned this costume/body and are in this scene. While it is being filmed, there are many "takes" until it is ready for the final reel. "Mis-takes" are just one of those "takes". They are the place you move on from. Later, when you replay the show, you'll recall those "mis-takes" and either laugh or cry while you notice where they led you. They were some of the most memorable parts of the production.

There are no mistakes worth hating yourself for. They are only springboards for success. "What you don't have, you don't need." is what a love of mine often said. It's true. See the beauty that you are; the unblemished bit of light that is shooting out of your eyes. This is truth.

Together we have found love – can you see it? It is right there, looking back at you from your mirror. It is you.

I am so grateful you are here with me.

I love you. Thank you.

Blasts from the Past

Day 1

This Quest began on February 14ᵗʰ, 2012, Valentine's Day.

"This Quest begins on a day set aside for loving and that is sort of akin to a fish setting aside a swimming day. You are loving all the time. Love doesn't look like any one thing or day, love is everything."

Day 5

"This week I witnessed a miracle. For six months I have been working with someone who openly disliked me. At least that was my interpretation of her hostility. Several days ago, she needed a favor and asked me, without agitation, for the first time. I complied, and then I did something I hadn't before. I sent her love and healing. I am sort of humbled to think I hadn't thought of this earlier, but I hadn't. I was mad and stubbornly refused to think of her in any way other than blameful – "She hates me and I don't know why."

A day passed and when I saw her next it was as if the light within had been switched on. Her eyes shone, she smiled, her hair was loose and we shared a moment. I felt amazing. A miracle.

There are no insignificant moments. There are no small acts of love. We are moving from polarity to unity. All of us together, are love."

Conditions

Prelude*

> This is a Quest for Love.
>
> Each day for a week, upon waking, look into a mirror.
>
> Find yourself there and look deeply into your own eyes once you do.
>
> Say "Hello. I love you."
>
> Say "There are no conditions in which I do not love you."
>
> Say "There is nothing that will stop me loving you."
>
> Now let that settle in your bones.
>
> Smile. Begin your day.

Welcome. Please follow along one day at a time.

This is not a race. Everyone wins on the Love Quest.

Day 1

Hello. It is day # 1 of your Quest.

If you are reading this, you recognize a need to love. It is not that you don't love. You do. It is that you have conditions in place that stop your loving.

On this Quest you are going to discover what is blocking your complete and unconditional love. You will root out and examine these things and then decide whether or not they serve you.

For you are love, you can't help but to love and love is what you do best. It is the whole point. You were loved into being and you are here, a piece of living, breathing love.

Love flows through you continuously. If it were allowed to flow, uninhibited, there would be no sadness or illness or fear or pain. Remember that "falling in love" feeling or that moment after exquisite sexual union? Both are delicious and overpowering and felt without restraint. You believe those feelings spring from another person or a specific activity. They are initiated through both but they exist within you always.

So why doesn't it last? Mostly, it is habit. Habit of emotion. You do not expect it to last and you always get what you expect. This is the way life works.

You are a walking, talking reservoir of love. The capacity for constant love is within you right now. The desire for continual love is also there. It is the belief that stops the flow, coupled with some addictive emotion that is not love.

You never learned how to love completely and without fear. As a tiny person – you began that way, but you have forgotten. Your elders taught you a falsehood – that you were imperfect and had to improve. Somewhere you took in the idea that you were not good enough. It is time to unlearn that idea and replace it with acceptance, understanding, kindness, patience and tenderness. Love yourself as you would an infant. Visually hold yourself with care and gently caress your sore heart.

The unloving addictions that are stopping the flow and blocking the spicket are not the point. What I mean by that is that they are not the focus. You will be successful when your gaze moves off of what is wrong about you and on to what is right about you. Everything about you is perfection.

Your life will show up as a string of repetitive reflections of whatever it is you believe.

Believe now the truth. You are a piece of glory, a strand in this tapestry of infinite beauty called life, and without you there would be a hole, an unfilled portion of perfection.

We need you and your love fully intact and expressed. We long for you. Love yourself without condition. This is why you are here.

See you tomorrow.

Day 2*

Hello. Welcome to your second day.

As a group we've learned similar, if not identical lessons around worth and worthiness. Underneath many of them is the notion that you must do something before you are good enough to receive something. You would call that something approval or acceptance or both. In my head, and from a very young age, these words sort of morphed into love.

I believed that if I did the right things, looked the right way, obeyed and performed when expected to, I would be loved. I somehow internalized the idea that you loved me when you were pleased with me and you didn't love me when you weren't. I also linked those ideas with attention so that my earliest decisions around love were that when you gave me "positive" attention you loved me and when you gave me "negative" or no attention, you didn't.

Perhaps your thoughts have been similar. My life became a series of actions designed in some part to get you to love me. I became a public servant. It is not wrong to serve the people, yet when that service becomes necessary for validation, it is counter-productive.

I am still a public servant, yet the difference is that now I always feel loved. I have learned that even when you are angry or yelling or unaware of me, you still love me.

How I got here was a gradual process of noticing, accepting and absorbing the judgmental and non-loving parts of me that were not making me happy. I do that still, as there are many.

The way to find out what is stopping you from feeling loved is to find something that makes you feel bad. Just one thing at first; a repetitive thing. What is that emotion that you recognize as "you"? When it rises up in you, is it familiar? You can feel it coursing through you as the heroin addict feels the drug travel through his veins after it is injected. This is your addiction. It is as powerfully addicting as heroin, make no mistake.

Mine is sad. It is another word for fear. Fear, as the opposite of love, has many names; anxious, jealous, tired, sick, angry, hurt, mad, frustrated, lonely, failure, wrong, bad, rejected, worthless, disappointed, weak, depressed, hate, angry, overwhelmed or unhappy. Anything that is not love is fear. In a sense, all of your addictions, at least the ones that stop you from loving, are the same. They are different versions of fear.

You have learned to be afraid. This Quest is not the place to root out how or why this has happened. This Quest is a way to discover and release it. When you find your addiction, don't reject it. It is you. It is a part of you that you've carried all these years for protection. Lovingly accept it.

I have a process that goes like this. When I have fallen into sadness, I first have to notice it is happening. It is so familiar that this is a tricky part. I don't see it right away as it has many disguises. Once I am able to see through them to sad, I conjure up a very clear image. It is me, as I look at that moment, in some state of miserable, of sad.

Next, I visualize a powerful and happy ME — usually dressed in an awesome outfit, strong and sure and joyful, and I approach "miserable me". I take her by the hands and look into her eyes and say — "I love you. This is not who I am anymore, I am love now." Then I hug her and as I do, she slowly becomes less and less dense, gradually dissolves and is absorbed into ME, the ME I am now (in the awesome outfit ;). This sometimes takes a very long time. I take her into ME because she is the precious beginning of who I am today.

Today, you are love. Today, the thing that has blocked you from seeing that love is every bit as imaginary as "time" *. You can move ahead as easily as you move your clocks. It is not that you have lost this part of you; it is that on this day, you've decided to move ahead, and to leave it where it is. It serves you now to operate with a new system, and fear does not work in this new "YOU". You may feel as if you lost something, and as it is an addiction, habit will try to replace it again and again.

Don't be fooled. The fear you've grown used to, is as arbitrary as time and you know that now.

Accept only love. In the construct of you, include one basic ingredient. It has many forms, shapes, sizes and sounds yet only one feeling – good. *When you feel good you've effectively moved into love.*

You are only love. *Everything else is just a way for you to see clearly; a backdrop of black so that your light can be sharp and clear and white and in focus.* You are okay. No performance or appearance is necessary for love to happen.

Love is here. It is you. Move into lightness of being. Smile. It's a new day and you've come to play. We are at your door, knocking, laughing and asking you to join us. You don't need to change anything, we know who you are and we love you, no conditions.

So, leave behind your reasons to say "no" and say "yes". We are waiting.

I love you. It is great to see you here. Thank you for showing up.

Day 3

What is holding up the love - is you. The world stands ready and waiting with adequate amounts of love to dispense. There is no problem with the equipment or the process or the supply. Everything is intact.

What prevents you receiving, feeling, and experiencing this love that is here for you, is merely your awareness of it. If you don't realize how easy to get and readily available something is, you will not see it as a possibility. On your Quest now, you have discovered it. Love is here for you. Actually, it is everywhere for you.

There is no need to wonder or worry about the love you've missed before this Quest. An immediate decision to recognize it changes everything.

Expect love. Accept nothing else. It is your expectation that defines your vision — you see what you expect to see and feel what you expect to feel.

It is okay to feel good, fantastic even. The familiar fears that prevent you from doing so are no longer necessary. *You've felt bad long enough.*

If you focus on how you feel, as the central point of any action you take around love, you will stay the course.

Others will show up, perhaps many others, to demonstrate to you your addictions. If you are addicted to "overworked", someone will show up to demand more from you. If your addiction is "abused" there will be one who abuses you in your life. If it is "low self-esteem" you'll find yourself in a situation you cannot succeed in, where you'll never feel good about the outcome. Do you understand? It is not that these others in your life are doing anything to you — it's that you are creating your life with your own set of tools, uniquely crafted to work in your hands only, and seen, felt and experienced by you alone.

Point of view is everything. Once you decide that everything is love, then that person who just said something unkind changes in your heart from "mean" to "misinformed". No one is out to get you. It is never their fault. It is just something that happened. The responsibility for how you feel about it is all on you.

Love yourself without restriction. You are more than you know, a physical expression of divinity, God in human form.

Nothing is wrong with you. You know now that those things that feel bad are just repetitive, addictive emotions. You can lovingly transform them into habits that serve you.

Love yourself as a matter of course. Inhale and exhale love as you do the air, for it is just as necessary to your existence. Self-love sustains you. It is your rock-solid core. Once discovered, it can no longer remain hidden. You know it is here now. Look in your eyes.

You are filled with love, made of love and surrounded by love. Every part of you that you discover on this Quest is love. Accept them all and your heart will be so full, you will feel an explosion of love. I am right here next to you, we all are, waiting for the overflow.

Thank you for joining this Quest.

See you tomorrow.

Day 4

You are halfway there.

I hope on this journey you are discovering what it is you are looking for. What you are searching for, is you. You are on a trip that will end where it began.

It is incredible really, the brilliance and perfection that is necessary for such a Quest. It was intricately set up by you, so that each aspect of yourself was hidden in plain sight. These parts of you have been walking with, talking with and breathing with you since you arrived. Cleverly disguised as us, they remain mysteries — until you wake up.

Awake now, you slowly notice yourself everywhere. It becomes painfully evident and inescapable. There is no one else out there. It's all you, reflected back time and time again; the beautiful and brilliant, bossy and bitchy, delicious and despicable. It's all you, all the time.

So, you want more love? I do. My cup has always room for more. When you love yourself, you can fill and refill it without having to go anywhere or depend on anyone. You must believe you are worthy.

In this search for self you will wade through your many hats – *to discover that the real you wears none.* When the hats are off, how do you describe what's left? Instead of introducing *your hats* to someone new (Mom, Dad, Writer, Teacher, Son, Daughter), you'll introduce *you* (Child of God, Bit of Perfection, Stardust, Love, Eternal Essence) Imagine the power and wall removing effect of this greeting,

"Hi. I'm a bit of Perfection, and you?" – or just, "Hi."

How would you respond?

This is not how you usually speak. Instead, you declare yourself with the style of your hat, and fall into the trap of names.

Naming things and people separates them. Necessary in a polarized world, in truth they are absent.

I have felt love. It is formless, nameless and unmistakable. I have felt unique souls both in and out of body and they are the same. Each soul was valued equally in my experience of them. Each was identified by their essence, their unique version of love.

With a blindfold on, you have embarked on a Quest for Agape. I do not know your social status, work title, nationality or religion. I only know I can feel you and, in that feeling, there is recognition.

You, like me, are a piece of Infinity; a version of divinity who has forgotten his way. You are stumbling around in the dark and when we crash into each other, you reach out and pull me up. In that moment I don't care how old you are or what you do for a living, what gender you are or how much money you have in the bank. It doesn't matter what your name is, where you live or who you pray to. In that moment, I can't see any of your hats but I can feel who you are. That is all I need to know. That is your truth.

As you stumble on your own Quest, remember to love yourself, regardless of what version you are looking at. Most of us close our eyes while hugging, I think because we recognize that it is a moment of union and is taking us beyond this physical realm. *What you see doesn't last while what you feel you never forget.*

As a fellow bit of Eternal Essence, I am honored to be in your presence. We have created together a sacred Quest. I love you absolutely. Treat yourself with reverence and care, for that is the only way to treat one such as you. Thank you for extending your heart out when I needed it, you have raised me up.

See you tomorrow.

Day 5

Welcome to the fifth day, the beginning of the second part of your Quest.

Today, take stock of where you are, how you feel, what is true and what feels real. Some days, love is easy. Others, not so much.

It is those other days I'd like to look at. Why do you have them?

In a polarized world there is contrast and you and I have set it up so that the one thing we really wanted to learn this time, we will run into again and again. There are many possibilities in moments, yet your addictions determine which you'll pick every time. As you clearly see the emotional "fixes" you are looking for, you can direct your actions and point the course of your moments in the direction of your greater intent. *This is consciousness.*

You must be gentle with yourself. Denial of love and acceptance, in any moment, is simply a denial of love. Keep in your heart and head the ultimate point of your life, of this Quest. You are shooting for love. Unconditional love means love without conditions. You are perfection.

There is nothing wrong about you. As you wake up, you will recognize the things about you that do not serve you. These are habits of emotion and once you notice yourself looking for another "fix", you can stop and move into another direction. This can be a challenge. It depends on the day, how you feel, what is going on around you and where you are.

One of my favorite things to do on some challenging days is to blame my "difficulty" on outside forces. This is, perhaps, slightly better than blaming my loved ones, as there is less potential for conflict, yet blame is never true. For me, as one who considers herself a sensitive in these intensely energetic times, I am always feeling something. There is a fine line between what is going on for me within and what I am picking up from the air and the people around me, (both seen and unseen ;). Regardless, my interpretation and subsequent reaction is all mine. Blame doesn't serve my intent.

In order to unconditionally love, it becomes necessary to peek around the blinders and see everything about yourself. *Clarity of vision may appear harsh, yet if it does, it is only because you harbor judgment.* It is all okay. What was once ugly and wrong is now just part of the whole, one of the choices.

Oneness and love are, in truth, one expression. This is understood at whatever spot you find yourself, yet our goal is identical. It must be, for you and I are one.

I do not look like you yet I know you. I feel the truth of you in my lovers embrace and this beautiful day. You are perfection. Hold onto that and know that you will also feel your perfection as truth one day. Maybe today.

This is where we are all headed actually, and although we'll arrive at different times, we will all, eventually, be here together.

We are practicing creation here, honing our skills. There is no one who knows better than you do and none more equipped. You are "fully loaded" to get the job done. Accept the version of you that shows up today, hug yourself and be who serves you.

The one you've been waiting for is you.

Thank you, for joining this Quest. I love you absolutely.

Day 6

Today is your sixth day.

I'd like to talk about expectations. For a very long time I believed that perfect love meant I got everything I wanted. How this looks in my head is that there are never any harsh words, betrayals of agreements or disappointments; my lover is faithful, my children are obedient and my friends and family always think I'm just great. I thought this meant happiness and that happiness meant love.

Yet I found that even on days when all those things happened, I was not happy. This made me wonder about love.

I understand now that love does not mean obedience or even loyalty in the sense that I am the only one loved. Love is something else. It is so easily misunderstood partly because of movies and stories that easily wrap things up in a specific amount of time or number of pages. We never see Cinderella and the Prince with four kids and a mortgage.

You are on this Quest because you are looking for love. Love is something that you know. It is a recognition that shoots through your body. It happens all the time, once you are aware of it. It could happen when your cashier says something to you, your child hugs you, or you meet eyes with a perfect stranger. It does not happen because your spouse takes out the garbage. That is appreciation. If your spouse never does so, it does not mean there is a lack of love.

Now taking the garbage out is a pretty innocent example, and deliberately so. Our spouses and lovers are subject to a host of expectations, of which garbage emptying may be one. Whether or not they fulfill those expectations does not indicate whether or not they love us.

Love is felt and expressed in your heart. You feel love. You sense love. If you expect love to look a specific way and spend your life looking for a specific face, body, job or action – you are bound to be disappointed.

Love is not predictable, but it is recognizable. Trust your heart. This does not mean you won't be disappointed from time to time. It means that regardless of where the relationship goes or went, you'll know what love is.

This is why we must love ourselves. In a unified existence, you start and end in the same place. Loving yourself - is loving me. If our connection is of a sexual nature we may engage in that for a bit, we may not. If it is creative in another way, we may collaborate on a project or other enterprise. Whether or not that happens does not determine the existence of the love. The love exists. It exists because you do. Love is what you are.

So, let go of expectations for perfection and expect love. You will never be disappointed.

I love you. See you tomorrow.

Day 7

You made it. You've reached the end of this Quest. Today is the final day.

We talked a bit about what love is and what love isn't. We've talked a bit more about these emotional addictions that you have that stop love in its tracks.

The trick now is to take some of these truths into your life. We've all been counseled or attended wonderfully transformative workshops that leave us feeling great for a few hours or days. Then, "real life" sets back in and we find ourselves struggling once again for answers, for more "quick fixes".

Love cannot be generalized – it is very specific. I cannot from these love notes reach in and identify your unique challenge. I can only share what I've learned and hope that you will be able to grab some of it and apply it in your life.

We are human together and as one we understand and share the concept of ego and agape. I would submit we have rarely seen the two co-exist.

Your ego is your very human self-definition. It is subjective and its goal is to keep you focused on your human part. This is a very small component of all that you are, yet this is the ego's job and it performs it very well.

Your ego, which is the voice of your addictions, wants to keep you focused here. When you chose to incarnate, your ego had an agenda; to make sure you stay the course and remain involved in your third dimensional life. The way to accomplish that is to preoccupy your mind with something, with an addiction.

You are so much more than the sum of your addictions. You have such a difficult time conquering them because this ego of yours is up to the task. The trick is not to reject your emotional addictions, but recognize, love, and alter them when they do not serve you. You can get addicted to "happy" or "strong" or "healthy". You were never told about the possibilities and you know better now. Loving yourself is paramount. It will give you the keys to the kingdom.

The signal that you've stepped into an addictive behavior is easy to spot – you feel bad. This is the only thing to remember. It is your sign that an addiction that doesn't serve you has taken over. Recognize it, visualize and love yourself – then tell yourself "This is not who I am anymore, I will stay here, no worries."

Then get addicted to something else and hug yourself.

Patience and persistence are required. Gentle acceptance and understanding will guarantee positive results. This is not a race and you are not out to win anything or beat anyone or reject any part of yourself. You are out to love. This is about agape.

You have been thinking all wrong about love and looking for it in all the wrong places. Love is not in your head, it resides in your heart. Love is recognized, not found as if it was lost. Love has been beneath your habits of fear. Fear has been all you could see and your addictions to fear all you could feed.

Your eyes are open now and you can see that love. It resides within you, within me, and everyone you know.

This shift is a shift from fear to love, separation to unity, and polarity to oneness. It is not a fantastic, esoteric, beyond your daily reality sort of shift. It is real and occurs for you while you are buying groceries, paying bills, watching news bulletins and caring for yourself. It is an internal shift, make no mistake.

In order for the changes you desire to occur, you have to love yourself. You are the one who is here. There is nothing you are, nothing you could think, say or do that is beyond love. Forgive yourself for every imagined fault and resolve to love. Just love.

Understand that you may be a work in progress but we all are and it is okay.

You are worthy. This life is your chance for you to love as a constant expression of who you are. The choices before you are love or fear. Choose love. You will always find there the answer you seek.

Thank you for joining this Quest.

I love you absolutely.

*Blasts from the Past

Prelude

This Quest took place in March of 2012, with the following invitation.

"This is a Quest for Love. Self-Love. It starts with you and ends with me and organically becomes US. We are one.
The Quest happens in your inbox. Each day for 7 days you will receive a note, examining some aspect of love. The note will also be posted on this page. As the week progresses, we will share our thoughts and experiences and we will help each other with love. As this journey progresses, we will explore self-love. Self-love is the answer to every question. You and I are one. As I understand and accept every facet of who I am, I cannot help but extend that understanding and acceptance out to you...and we have unity. Oneness.
This Quest will explore what is halting our progress. What sorts of road blocks prevent us from loving? It may not be what you think.
The Shift starts there. We cannot hope to move from polarity to unity with requirements and conditions and blame filling our minds. We cannot move forward with fear. It is love that will create this Shift. Our goal is agape.

For love is always true. What may be confusing us is our definition of love. Love needs no definition. Love is what you are. See you on the Quest."

Day 2

"In the U.S. we set our clocks ahead, and in real "time" we lose an hour. Since childhood, I have always wondered where it went. We rely on our timepieces to regularly record and report the passing of "time" and yet on this one day most of us just push it forward. I believe our universal agreement to do this — to manually adjust something so seemingly rock solid as "time", only stands as evidence that we are collectively making this all up. This is a dream. It will go as we say it goes."

Habits

Prelude*

Today begins another Quest.

Each day for one week you will meet yourself in the mirror.

Not the disheveled, just out of bed and sort of a mess you. The real you.

Look in your mirror upon waking.

Say "Hello there."

Wait for a moment and see what you say back to yourself.

If there is judgment in your answer, smile. Let it go.

Keep looking. You are starting to find yourself. You are in there, behind your eyes.

Say "It is good to find you where I left you."

Say "I love you."

Feel that.

Now carry that with you as you begin your day.

Welcome. Please follow along one day at a time.

This is not a race. Everyone wins on the Love Quest.

Day 1

You are looking for that which you are. It may be that others see it, yet you yourself must see it now. You know it is there and believe it to be truth. Yet it must be felt to be *known. It must be known to be felt.*

You've heard that you are love and if you believe the words, you know. Now it is time to feel it. You are out to feel the love that you are.

Your Quest will not take you beyond yourself. Love starts with you. It ends with you. Love is always and all ways you.

Start with the mirror. Look into your own eyes. Really look. Who do you see there? Your challenge as you start this journey is to look until you see what's real. What is real is not your skin or your hair color or eye color, but you. For what you are is nothing less than divine. See the light in your eyes. It is that light that will show you the way.

You are not alone. You are not wrong. You are not weak. You are One. Do you see? This Quest is a game. You are hiding from yourself; pretending to be somewhere other than where you are. You are here, now; all of us expressions of love, together, looking for ourselves.

It starts with acceptance and looks like forgiveness. Begin with that you in the mirror; who so desperately wants your love and who needs you to cherish who he or she is. You are perfection.

Reflections of Source shoot out from your eyes. Can you see them there? It is the light that I seek when we meet; this is the juice that replenishes everyone you gaze at.

You are my inspiration, the propulsion behind my words. In you I see the physical expression of life. From you I feel the love that sustains me.

This is why you are here. Do you see in your eyes, the answer? Trust what you know.

That quiet moment when all is well, this is who you are. Your questions and problems and flaws and mistakes are not errors to be hated but necessary steps to be appreciated. You have all the answers and none of them are incorrect.

Love yourself without condition. Begin your journey to Love. Know that you are beautiful and beyond any doubt. You are Love. We could not be here without you, thank you.

I love you.

See you tomorrow.

Day 2

You are here to love. What has stopped you from loving *is yourself.* You have not purposely done this. It is your habit; these are just your habits of emotion. These habits are like lead weights on a bird – with them you cannot fly.

You were taught by your elders from infancy. Your responses to life began the moment you arrived. Each event and every response elicited a reaction from society. You gauged yourself accordingly. Habits were born. They seemed to work at the time.

You are all grown up now. After a lifetime of being fed a specific diet, you have come to expect it. If it is not in your immediate view, you'll create it. These habits are no less powerful than any substance addiction, and you can get them anywhere. You don't need a drink or a chemical for this fix; you need a situation. Your days our filled with them.

If you are here, there is a question from deep within that sounds like – "Why don't I feel good all the time?" Your habits of emotion prevent you, they are meant to stop you from flying.

You came to this earth with a plan. As an incredibly powerful being of light, you slowed yourself down in order to have this very human experience. You have come to learn – to experience every facet of existence. You contracted with your family, friends, loved ones and associates to help each other along the way. *Yes – help*. Those that challenge, hurt and annoy you are your closest loves. You are connected. You challenge, hurt and annoy them too. That's how it works.

You grew up with specific levels of emotion in your days. It is this that you know as equilibrium. You feel "out of sorts" if your days don't provide enough stress of some sort *or enough of a specific emotion*.

The ego you developed is not wrong; it is doing its job. It is supposed to keep you focused on this 3D earth, via your emotional response to life. You became so wrapped up in these emotions, that you never questioned them. They provide your expectations, and as such they create your life.

Do you see? Things feel weird when I haven't been really sad for a while. I will "run into" a story that has no immediate bearing on my life and I fall apart; this destroys my day. I snap at my co-workers, yell at my cat, and burn dinner. Now I can feel *really bad* and guilty too. This goes on for days – I pile on the evidence and I have forgotten the immediate story that triggered this spiral – my self-esteem is shattered. Eventually life does not even seem worth it. I feel unloved and pointless.

This story, with some personal touches, may sound familiar. Your ego is not out to get you. It is not wrong. Yet, you are on a Quest. A Quest for Love. You have a different agenda now.

In order to alter the responses that spring from ego, and succeed on your Quest for Love, persistence is necessary. You see, your ego wants to keep you here, embroiled in your dramas so that you "get" your lessons.

Now though, you want to fly. It is time to let the habits go, drop the drama, release the addictions. You have come now with wings that are all grown in — full and powerful. It is time to soar.

There is nothing wrong with you and no one at fault. Everyone has had their part to fill. This is a new game. Everybody wins.

Love every moment you've been given and every part you've played. Each has been necessary to get you to this point. You are here to demonstrate love in physical form. **Look in the mirror. This is what love looks like.**

You are the one you've been waiting for.

See you tomorrow.

I love you.

Day 3

So today let's go someplace else. This is a place of your deepest longing. It is where our hearts reside, beating as one, drawing us ever closer. Agape.

What does it mean to love yourself? Does it happen once you win the game, lose the weight, fill your bank accounts and save the world? There is no time or condition in which agape occurs — it is now.

Loving yourself does not require perfection, traditional beauty, wealth or status. Loving yourself requires trust. That's it. There is a you beneath your outfit and your anger, your errors and your trophies, your humor and your tears. Trust your truth.

You will find it in this place of love. Beneath the demands and requirements of ego, your love waits. It has been waiting a long time.

This place is cushioned with gentility. There is room here for everyone. This is what heaven looks like.

Here there is no judgment. You are welcome as you are, perfect where you stand. Your truth is all we see here. It is your light that shows the way.

What's surprising is how familiar this feels. These walls look just like the ones in your home, on a street that bears the same name as the one you now live on. What's up with that?

There is no place to go. There is nothing to do. There is only acceptance.

Imagine today you are in this place of love. Within these walls all is good. You are okay. You are spoken to gently, loved absolutely, cherished. In this place all is known. There are no secrets here. Every facet of your life is on the table and still the flow does not diminish. It is palpable, this love. You are engulfed in adoration, awash in tenderness. Joy is evident when you enter here. This is home.

Here is where you are headed. It doesn't matter where else you've been or what you did when you got there. This is home.

Without condition love who you are. No more waiting. This Quest has only one destination – agape. It is love that will take you there and acceptance that will direct your path. You have to walk there yourself – this is a place you cannot be taken – you have to go. On your own.

Love yourself without condition. This is the way to agape.

I love you.

See you tomorrow.

Day 4

It is your fourth day. You've reached midpoint. You've come so very far and seen what awaits you when you finally arrive. Knowing what you do now, you wonder why you haven't jumped on the expressway to get there as soon as possible. What's with all these detours, scenic routes and vehicle breakdowns?

They are the composite parts of this trip. Without them, you'd be bored. You were not born there, you have to get there. This is life.

It is the drama you love so much, the variety, the ups and downs, thrills and chills of pain and pleasure. As Bill Hicks said "It's just a ride." It's a ride you stood in line a long time to take. Many are still waiting – yet you are here.

To enjoy this ride, you have to remember it's short lived and temporary and a ride you wanted to take. You intended to get off at some point, richer for the experience. You will survive – *you are not the ride, you are ON the ride.*

That distinction makes all the difference. When you have an unloving thought or disempowering idea, remember its part of the ride, and has never been true. You've entered the "Illusory Zone", where things are not as they seem. Stay as long as you want; just don't forget you are on a ride. What is true is that you are pure love, a piece of divinity; all rolled up in human form. There is nothing else that defines you completely. You are, for now, wearing this human suit. It temporarily looks right, wrong, weak, strong, holy, unholy, criminal, saintly, rich, poor, young, old, happy or sad.

This is all costuming and it makes for a better show. The deep unhappiness you feel is because you've believed your own show; you forgot this was just a ride.

This time now is one for truth – you are waking up – you are more than you've been told. The power you hold is immense – you have sprung from Source. Embrace your truth, it is love that will propel you, agape that fuels you.

Once you accept the fact of your divinity, miracles occur. The detours and illusions of doubt and despair must be seen for what they are – they are false. Gently speak to them your truth, tell them they have served you, the trip has been interesting, but you are no longer in need of their services.

See yourself whole and strong, filled with light and love. This is your truth. This magnificent-you is waiting with open arms – it is time to step into them.

It is an honor to be on this journey together.

See you tomorrow.

Day 5

So, you are on a roll... beginning your downhill part of the journey now. You are entering the last part of the excursion. This is where things get interesting. Sometimes, when you head down, it is scary. It seems to move really fast and you don't always feel in complete control. There are even times you may question your own sanity – "why did I ever say I would do this?"

Right now, there may be some pretty intense moments on your trip. They are only there to show you how strong you actually are. This is "stuff", this is scenery, this is drama, this is the part where you gather your internal resolve and be the best you possible. Your moment to shine has arrived. Pretend that you are a being of light, and when the challenge shows up and habits pull strong, think to yourself, "what would a being of light do right now?"

I have done this. I find myself thinking old thoughts, thoughts of complaints, problems, sadness, "oh, woe is me" sort of thoughts, drama stuff. This is not life or death that is bringing this on... this is just daily sort of regular "problems". Then, (when I remember to do so), I think, *"What would a being of light do right now?"*

Immediately I sit straighter. Sometimes, I change my clothes and even put on some makeup, (smile). Mostly, I just feel the truth of me. I feel stronger. I feel worthwhile. I remember that it was me who said I would do this thing, or who chose this person to work with or to love with or buy from or whatever. I feel my power and my words come out clearer than before. I don't hear any more complaining in my ears, I don't see anything to complain about – I see there is something to do, and I do it. I ask for help and I don't feel weak for doing so. I see myself as worthy of loving.

I will repeat that. *See yourself as worthy of loving. As soon as you do, you are.*

There is nothing but good in you. What is happening these days is you are going through a "sorting". If this was a Harry Potter movie, there would be a magic hat and it would be apparent to all which house you belonged in. The sorting now comes from within. You are in control. You are putting these situations in front of yourself so that you choose clearly. There will be no mistakes here. You need to make a choice.

Will you love yourself? How fast will you head towards agape? How many dead ends will you go down before you sail on clearly to love? It is up to you. You are an amazing creature, here to pave the way for untold numbers of us as we trudge along this path to oneness/love/agape.

I am grateful for your journey, as it helps me on mine. We are here together to share. Perfection is an assemblage of flaws... together we are beautiful, exquisite even. We need you. There is no singular or specific way to come to love. There is only your way. Trust yourself.

You are the one you have been searching for, waiting for.

Thank you for sharing this trip with me. I love you.

See you tomorrow.

Day 6

Let's talk about the miraculous. It is what occurs when self-doubt stops talking.

The voice in your head is the voice of your emotional addictions. It has spoken without conscious direction for your entire life. It is the voice of judgment, doubt and worry.

When we were children we used our inside voices when we were in office buildings and institutions and our outside voices when in the playground. It is time to change this "addiction voice" (used in both places) into a voice that serves you everywhere. When a criticism or doubt or worry speaks, gently tell it no, you no longer need this particular advice. You are good, (in fact, you are great.).

What you will find once the "negative ego" voice quiets down, is that there is silence. It gets very peaceful in there and this can be quite disconcerting; you now have room for the miraculous. This is where the magic happens.

Internal pre-occupation stops us from self-love and empowerment. Agape paves the way for wonders. Without all that noise, lots of things occur. You may notice energy, things you haven't seen before. This silence for a moment or six may have you experiencing visions. Beings from other dimensions may become visible. Life gets interesting if you let it.

This does not require any extra power, only a belief in who you actually are – an acceptance of your divinity. You are love, a moment of magnificence here on the planet now to usher in a new age – the Age of Enlightenment. It promises to be a great ride.

As my own voice got quieter I began to experience psychic and "other world" phenomena, visions and what we would term "miracles". It was not so much that I did anything to make this happen; it was that my eyes had room to see them now and my head had space to process what I was seeing. This is interesting and fun yet the most fun is the very third dimensional creation of every day miracles – those that involve the daily stuff and people in our lives.

Loving yourself just gets rid of static. One who loves themselves without condition will not stand for berating or doubting themselves. Once you accept your own divinity you can start to command your own life. At first it was things like green lights and parking places and always arriving on time.

You have to believe that it was not chance but **100% YOU** that created each in order for it to continue. A quiet mind allows you to approach each parking lot with intent. There may be, at first, just one out of 3, 5 or even 10 that gets you that prime parking spot, yet eventually with consistent, unwavering belief – it is 10 out of 10.

What happens is that when the quiet shows up you need to fill it in. As humans, our tendency is to create. We have to create SOMETHING. This is why we are here, it is what we do. Now you can create consciously, with love, honor and respect. *This is how a being of light lives on earth.*

Once you arrive at places on time and park in front, expect a perfect day. I usually intend the highest and best for all concerned and *visualize everyone satisfied and happy at the end.* Do this with errands, days at work, dates and parenting. Fill your life with miracles. It will become a stream of seamless joy, and there will be plenty of room for you to manifest your dreams. This is how life was meant to be lived.

Begin today with love. It is you who holds the answers; you are here to show the way. Love yourself without condition and then expect the magic. You hold it within your heart.

I love you where you stand.

See you tomorrow.

Day 7

You are here. You have completed your Quest, today marks the final day. You are different today than when you began. You can see just a bit more clearly the alternative paths, the detours, dead-ends and super highways available to you. Your eyes have opened a bit wider; you see things differently today.

For *what is all around you is what your belief has put there*. This is truth. If I believe I am love, then I will only see those that love me. There may be some that dislike me, argue with me, call me a dreamer or foolish, and that's okay. I know that I am love and that they are love and that one day, their eyes will open to the love that they are. When that happens, they too, will behold a loving world.

When you understand and believe the love that you are, your world changes. No longer do you take anything personally. No longer do you defend or argue, as you realize that those engaging that way are merely arguing and defending themselves, not attacking you. You are not better or worse than they are. You understand another perspective; a broader view. It holds only beauty.

You will begin to see the magnificent in the ordinary. You will not be separate from others, not by a long shot. You will be a part of every other one of us. This life you are living, this journey to love, is extraordinary, filled with light and vibrating pure love. It is exquisite and exciting and just plain fun.

Even when it isn't. There are times when the journey gets to be a challenge. This is where you test your metal, for you will never know how strong you are until tension is applied. It will be. It has to be; we would be bored otherwise. All of us have our own tests, our own drama, and our own pain. This is not to make light of whatever shows up for you or is there for you right now. This is to say, it's okay, it's going to be all right, you are love and you have come to show the way. As you move through each crisis and heartbreak and challenge, you will grow ever stronger and convince yourself of your own truth. You are love.

Remember who you are. In the coming days and weeks, remember your light. When you find some empty, quiet space in your head, visualize the moment, parking place, day or life of your dreams. Keep on doing this. You'll see. Whatever shows up is there for the learning. See it not as a failure, but another step on the way. You are headed for miraculous. The really cool part is that once you get there, you will only then notice that there are other places to go.

For this journey does not end. I submit that you are only at the beginning, and that once you realize your truth, your divinity, your power and your love, you begin to truly live. This is the life you came to experience, indeed to create. You are the one you have been waiting for.

Until we meet again, love yourself without condition.

*Blasts from the Past

Prelude

This is the invitation from April 2012.

"This is a Quest for Love. Self-Love. It starts with you and ends with me and organically becomes US. We are one.

This month we will look at how pervasive and persistent our habits of emotion are. We will learn how to use the doggedness of our nature and ego to our advantage and discover how miracles happen. They happen with love. We are the miracle makers and we have the magic. It is us.

As this journey progresses, we will explore self-love. Self-love is the answer to every question.

The Shift starts there. We cannot hope to move from polarity to unity with requirements and conditions and blame filling our minds. We cannot move forward with fear. It is love that will create this Shift. Our goal is agape.

For love is always true. What may be confusing us is our definition of love. Love needs no definition. Love is what you are.

See you on the Quest."

Conviction

Prelude

This Quest again asks you to forgive.

Each day, for one week, you will contemplate and then offer forgiveness.

When you wake up in the morning, remember.

Remember who you are, and what you must do.

Look into your mirror, find your own eyes.

Smile with those same eyes.

Say "Hello."

Say "I love you."

Say "I forgive you."

Keep looking and smiling until you feel that you mean it.

Take that acceptance with you as you embark on yet another Quest.

It will offer you a place in which to trust others.

Allow these others into your heart with acceptance.

Now forgive them. Forgive all of them.

Realize that they are merely mirrors of your own internal dialogue.

Love them. Have a remarkable week.

Welcome. Please follow along one day at a time.

This is not a race. Everyone wins on the Love Quest.

Day 1

Things are changing with increasing speed. Depending on where you are focused, you are witness to some sort of upheaval. Whether personal or global, the things we've counted on no longer seem to work.

There is one thing that will sustain you; agape. You are here to understand and finally realize your own divinity. For countless years you've been playing a game. You've been willing participants; it has taken its toll. You've even forgotten that it's a game.

It is vital now for you to remember. There is no one other than you who can do this. There is no one other than you for you to forgive. All that you see is a mirror. All that you see is yourself.

Love yourself; gently, persistently, relentlessly and continuously. There is no other. There is only you.

Source wanted to know itself through experience and you were loved into being. There is nothing you can do to disappoint source. There is nothing you can do that is beyond love's reach.

You are divine. Every negative thought is a contrast point for you to realize your truth. Love yourself.

In times of uncertainty, remember these things. You chose and were chosen to be here now. This is not the time to give up; it is the time to believe. These words are not new yet these times are unprecedented. Each hurdle seems insurmountable.

You came to do this. You are here to love. There is no one with your outlook, your unique brilliance – besides you. We are one and your part is necessary to our completion. Look at your hands, your feet, your body – it's you; wonderful, perfect and complete.

Know that these many, many years you've been intentionally led to believe you were less than you are. Realize now the truth of you. Reach into your good strong heart and find your center. From there you will emerge whole and complete and unstoppable.

It is good to be together again.

You are the one you are waiting for.

Day 2

Welcome to your second day.

You are here to locate love. It is not lost; it has just been forgotten. The intentional minimizing of its importance has left its mark. You may believe that some part of you, or something you have said or done is not worthy of love. If there is just one thing you could do to change the world, it would be to let that go.

Imagine a planet filled with people who know who they are and who love who they are. See the light emanating from everyone's eyes and the smiles brightening every street corner. This is a world populated with beings of light.

This, in a very real sense is earth. Only we've covered our light with despair and frustration and requirements and fear. It doesn't matter why or how it's been covered. It matters that we notice the light that still exists. Be assured that all of our brilliance has been dimmed. It is time for you to shine.

Confidence comes from knowing your part. You've had lifetimes of rehearsals for this. You sense internally that something big is happening. It is — you are here to step into the light. You have come to live as the love that you are.

As you tentatively emerge there will be a culling – "Is this what love looks like?" will be the question again and again.

Love is not necessarily agreement. It is not disagreement either. Love is the freedom to choose. There is no control in love – people may not always do what you want them to. This doesn't mean there is not love. You are not here to agree with everyone, you are here to love everyone.

There are indications that we are about to be told of some truths from our past. As these emerge it is our job to just love. The darkness that held the planet was evidenced in every facet of it; criminal behavior, self-hatred, corruption, pollution, war, blame and judgment.

You are here to usher in the light. As you love yourself without condition, you raise the vibration of the planet and her people. There are no exceptions. Love is appropriate in every situation. The power of our unified love is beyond anything you've yet seen. It is liberating an entire world.

There is nothing more important than self-love. It is the thing we can all do. You don't need to worry about convincing anyone else. Your audience is the mirror. Unity means that from there, all of life is altered.

All of life responds to your love. We are One. As you accept yourself as perfect, I become okay too. I am so very grateful for your love; you have allowed me to accept myself. Thank you.

At your core is love. When something happens to reach that part of you, it is undeniable. It could be a hug, a moment, a word or a handshake – the jolt to your center is confirmation. Trust. You know who you are. You know what you've come to do.

Let no one, no situation or seeming crisis deter you from your purpose. You are here to love. You have come to share your truth.

We are together dispelling the darkness with our collective light.

We are the ones we've been waiting for.

Day 3

Welcome to your third day. You are on this journey to consider and discover love.

This specific Quest is about conviction. Conviction is defined as a strong belief. It is in this time now that the trust of your deeply known beliefs is paramount. You know your own heart.

Love has been heralded and demonized, recognized and ignored, blamed and honored. With the multitude of songs, movies, books and poetry it is undeniably our most popular subject; hence the confusion.

Although it may not be completely understood love is known. You may not be able to define it to your satisfaction, but you sure can recognize it. Love is a feeling. It is a noun. It is a verb.

There is no such thing as wrong love. Love does not dissipate; once you love someone, they are forever with you. Love sometimes looks like something else. You have to feel love to know when it is there. Love doesn't always make sense.

We are infinite beings, having an endless number of experiences. In your life here now, you've come to participate in a beautiful moment.

Many of us are here. There is a chance for you to bump into more than one "soul mate" as we move through these times. You will know — the instant recognition verifies your connection. You may be associates, friends, lovers or just push each other's buttons, but there is no denying the force that joins you. It's all love.

Trust whatever it is you feel deep within — you know the truth. You were born with it, lived a life being told otherwise and now have the opportunity to act on it with conviction.

Love is okay regardless of who you feel it for; a kitten, a baby, a lover or a stranger. It is never wrong. Rightness or wrongness implies some sort of judgment. You do not, nor will you ever, know precisely what someone else is feeling or thinking. An accurate judgment about someone else's thought process is a fallacy. The only one you know, and know absolutely, is you.

This is a time to release your concern over what others are thinking. There is no one else to worry about; we are all in this together. Focus on your heart and do what feels right. It is. Trust.

As your actions and words spring from that very core part of you, you gain confidence and conviction. As others witness your strength, it ripples out and we are all strengthened.

You are love and together we are deciding the direction of our civilization. When we hit the right note, our harmony will be heard throughout the universe.

We are the ones we are waiting for.

Day 4

You are at the midpoint of your Quest. On this particular Quest, you will determine your tensile strength. This will tell you how much you can bear without pulling apart.

For as much as love is about you, it is about me; and as much as love is about me, it is about every other being and organism sharing this life with you. Love is what you are, and you are here now, practicing love in physical time. In order to understand what love is capable of, you must experience resistance.

For the rest of your journey, tension will be applied abundantly. You will be surrounded with mirrors; facing yourself repeatedly. Over and over they will ask – "Do you love me now?", "Am I worth your time?", "Have you heard me?", "Do you love me now?", "Are you listening?", "Do I matter?", "Can you hear me?", "Do you love me now?"

Understand that this is a circle, it always returns to the beginning; it starts and ends with you. There are no exceptions to this. Life, creation, love – all work this way.

You are moving from polarity to unity. Sometimes it will be seamless and painless and wonderful. Other times it won't. In those times remember – everyone is right and everyone is love. Each soul's version is worthy of expression.

By divine decree you are here to express life. Each of us puts forth a unique version of love and that love is then experienced by Source. You are perfect and so is everyone else. If we are going to collaborate and create a new earth, all of us must be heard. The test of our tensile strength begins now.

There are dramas and stories in your personal relationships. This is your proving ground. With acknowledgement and consideration and an open heart the strength of your love will carry you through beautifully. You know who you are. It is time to be. It is time to walk your talk. No exceptions.

You are the one you are waiting for.

Day 5*

Welcome to your fifth day.

As you love yourself your world changes. Let not another day pass without reinforcing agape. Today, look in the mirror, into your own eyes and tell yourself "I love you. You are doing a great job." Wrap your arms around your shoulders and squeeze. Feel the love that you are. This is something you can hold on to, no matter what happens. This is the core truth, the one that has been kept from you for so very long. You are love.

The love that you are is an infinite expression of divinity. Once you reinforce that truth with a hug – just be. Every moment you are love. Everywhere you go, you bring love. This is not a small part of you, this is your source. What would love do now?

What would love do now? Love is what you are, and this "you" is much bigger than you know. Act is if you love all that you are. Pay attention. When you look in your eyes and declare your love – ask "What can I do?" "How can I love you?"

What your eyes see, is you. What your ears hear, is you. It's all you.

You are bigger than you know. It is time to love the world you have created. Expand. Your love is huge. Treat all of it as a priceless piece of art. Your body, your mind, your heart, your soul, your lover, your family, your neighbors, your community, your world – it's all you.

We have been led to believe we are small. It is a lie. Love is not a pie with each piece taking away from the whole – love is a garden. Giving a piece does not take away from anyone. Giving only multiplies and our collective garden becomes paradise. It is time to step out of our frightened heart and spread the love that you are. It is time to work for the light. This is who you are.

You are the one you are waiting for.

Day 6

It is your sixth day. On this journey, you've begun to explore what it is to live as if you are love. This is huge. It is not just that you pat yourself on the back and then proceed with your day in self-hatred. It is that you carry that embrace with you. In every moment you are love. In every instant you are perfection. Nothing that you face today will diminish the glory of you. There are none worthier, none more divine and none more magnificent.

Live this way. A being such as you now walks the earth. You... You are here to demonstrate love. There is no other with your unique version of divinity. This is your moment.

Each day, validate your worth. Do it with post-it notes, say it to the mirror, sing to yourself, dance with abandon. You have been through so much. For most of your time here you've believed what you were told. In error you thought you were imperfect and undeserving.

Now that you know, never let it be forgotten. You are love. Agape is the single most powerful thing you can embrace. Love yourself.

You've planned and performed your life flawlessly. You are here, now, in these times and at this moment, to bring to life the truth.

We will all benefit when you step out of your safety net and show us who you are. We could not do this without you.

Live as if you were the greatest thing on earth. You are. Your heart holds the key to unparalleled joy. Open it. Let us in.

You are the only power you need. Connect to Source through your love. It is all around you — the people, the birds, the trees, the earth — we are all waiting, humming, getting ready to sing full out.

The strength of our collective voice has never been heard — let's make it known. It begins in your heart, looking into your own eyes, trusting and believing in your own feelings. The Creator didn't get it wrong when you were birthed. It was a genius moment. You are a brilliant bit of light, here to illuminate us all.

You are the one you've been waiting for.

See you tomorrow, as you complete your Quest.

Day 7

You made it. Your journey ends today. It is as if something has broken through. Today begins anew.

You know now that you are love – you may be man, woman, twenty, sixty, American, African, tall, short, doctor or dancer – yet we are the same. Our unity exists in our soul. We began as one thought – love – and that thought never changed.

This transformation is happening everywhere. We have found each other to remind ourselves of truth; because here we come only from our heart, and it is our hearts that beat as one.

Know that when you gaze into your eyes each morning, you are seeing all of us. Treat yourself with care; you are a sacred object, a piece of the divine, a treasure. Be gentle with your heart. There is only one of you here now and your love is needed.

For whatever else you are – you are first and foremost a spark of love. This is the footprint you will leave on this earth. For nothing else matters in the final analysis. You will be remembered for how you loved.

Love with abandon. We are in interesting times and they seem to get wilder with each day. What you can hang on to, when everything else changes, is the spark within. Your light will show the way.

Let go of your judgments and refuse any guilt. It is a new day and you are here with something only you can give. We cannot successfully navigate this life without your contribution. We are one.

You may not do or be exactly what you expected and that's okay. As you let go of the "shoulds" your true self emerges. You emerge steadfast and true and what you have to give is vital.

Trust that inner voice, prompting you forward. Love yourself without hesitation. You are okay. In fact, you are a delight. The urge to be you was so strong that our creator couldn't resist. Here you are. Wonderful, gorgeous, individual you – a masterpiece created with a master's touch.

I love you absolutely.

Thank you for sharing this journey.

*Blasts from the past

Day 5

"This has been an interesting, rather intense time to hold a Love Quest. The shifting energetic levels create a surreal light and sensation in my last few days. I have gone from being deeply fatigued to experiencing a sort of "sparkler effect" throughout my body, sort of shooting out my limbs.

I believe the light right now is becoming somehow sort of visible. In my home, the lighting is different. The color is not the same and there is no explanation for it – all fixtures and bulbs are the same.

Last night, we were in our backyard and for a few moments a very deep neon orange/red light painted a path through the trees and houses. It looked the same way it does when the city marks a tree for removal, there was no bleeding of the colors, it was like a splash of solid color. We could not find its source. (spaceship?) (smile)."

"As this year moves into its second half, (this was June Of 2012) and we watch the events transpire, there is one theme that predominates. It has been in my head for weeks now and may be in yours as well. It can be summarized in one word – "waiting".

I woke up today with some ideas about that ... We are not waiting for the light. We are the Light. We are light workers. What does it mean to be a light worker? It means we work to bring the light. Waiting is not necessary."

Adoration

Prelude*

Begin this Quest as you have each of the previous ones, with love.

Each day for 7 days, look in your mirror first thing in the morning.

Say "Hello there."

Say "I love you."

Say "Yes, I really, really love you."

Say "In fact, you are my favorite person ever."

Let that sink in, while you continue to gaze into your own eyes.

This is the beginning of adoration. This is how you are loved by Source.

Have a great week.

Welcome. Please follow along one day at a time.

This is not a race. Everyone wins on the Love Quest.

Day 1*

Hello. Welcome to your Quest for Agape.

This time you will explore deeply the truth of your connection – oneness. For as One, we are beginning to appreciate just what that actually means. Agape takes on a whole other "dimension" when you understand that the One you unconditionally love – is us.

When you understand deeply this truth, you find something that may surprise you. It is okay to love yourself. In fact, it is necessary. *For what is held in your head about this being that is you, will radiate out to become your entire world.* This life that is yours is a projection of whatever it is you believe. What you believe, you perceive.

Believe in yourself. You chose and were chosen to be here today. You are the Master, it is not necessary to seek truth in another, you only need remember. You are love. A God particle shot from Source, here to love in the darkest place in the universe. Earth has been your home not as punishment or because we are lesser beings, but because we are brilliant lights.

Only one such as you could handle this dimension and this planet at this time. Only light such as yours is brilliant enough to sustain itself while immersed in ideologies of war, greed, subservience, slavery, illness and pain. Not only have you maintained – you have become a beacon of light and altered the course of humanity.

Our favorite movies are those in which the odds are clearly stacked against the lead character and he or she triumphs anyway. This is because we've been watching our future, writing our own story, and remembering why we are here. Every thought, word, and deed, whether self or other directed is a line in the script. You know this truth today. It is time to write each line with one focus – love. This is why you are here. Intend only love.

Your power is unmatched. We are surrounded with off world beings not to help us so much as to watch us. We are transforming ourselves and the planet on which our feet are parked, with not much more than our faith to go on. Your inner promptings have led you here, to a place of choice.

In the sharp contrasts you encounter each day, you see clearly the options; to see yourself as separate and judge or to see yourself as One and love. What you do, think, and feel in each moment becomes your life.

Love yourself. Give yourself a gift today. Begin this Quest with immersion in adoration. Take a walk, a few extra moments and honor the One that is you. He is beautiful beyond description. She is powerful beyond measure. You are the Master of the Universe. Uni-Verse. One Verse. One Song. Us.

There is no other here to sing this song. It is you.

You are the one you've been waiting for.

See you tomorrow.

Day 2*

Welcome to your second day.

You know what it is to love. You've got this. Imagine being accepted completely, loved with abandon and held in the highest regard. You are. You are deserving of tenderness, honor and respect. You are a piece of God, a fragment of divinity and the holder of all good things. This is how you are seen and loved right now.

There is no line to stand in to wait for this reward and no good or special behavior is necessary. This is not something to be earned – this is what you are.

Source energy breathed you into being and whispered "Go forth, my magnificent one, and light the places where darkness has taken over. I hold you in the highest regard. You are my emissary, and I trust you to love without reservation all of my creation – first and foremost you."

You are adored. There is nothing you can do to disappoint Source – nothing will diminish the love that is yours. Your deepest secrets and "worst" offenses are what makes you, you. You have made no mistakes; you've merely made choices from whatever perspective you held at the time. It's all okay and was part of your plan.

And what was your plan? To emerge from the darkness and show us the way. Source so loved and trusted the one in your mirror that all of life was placed gently in your hands.

This is because you know what it is to love. You have felt the tug on your heart strings when looking into the eyes of your loved one. You have embraced each other and shared unconditional loving. In the moment of love's recognition, there are no rules. In that secret place, where hearts reside, there is only love, only "yes".

This is how you love. Hold nothing back and offer no exception – you are perfection.

Take yourself to the mirror and gaze into your own eyes – look deeply and find your core. He is there. She is waiting. All along they have known this moment would come. It is here.

Feel the love that you are. Know that Source runs through each particle of you and honor every centimeter. You are sacred and hold within all the power and love that exists. It is compressed into one being – you. You are carrying out the plans of the creator; actualizing love in a sea of fear.

You are right on time and ready for this. Your light just gets brighter and more of us are illuminated each day.

Thank you for joining us, it is great to be together again.

We are the ones we've been waiting for.

Day 3

It is your third day.

If you and I are One, then how I am seeing and thinking about you, is also how I am seeing and thinking about me. Every opinion is a condition; every judgment, a lack of love.

We are on a Quest for Agape, reaching for unconditional love. Why? Because within Agape are the keys to the kingdom. Therein rests the answer to every question.

There is no problem that does not boil down to fear or lack of love. There are no other solutions necessary but one. Love is all you need.

Fall in love with yourself. You are fundamentally connected to every bit of life that you are aware of. There is nothing separate from you. What does it mean to love the One that we are?

It means words like cherish, respect, tenderly, gently, carefully, patiently and willingly each describe the ways you interact with the people, plants, pets and life around you. There is only one answer and it is yes. Every bit of life you bump into is another opportunity to love; another bit of you.

Just when you think you've accepted yourself, you find that you are face to face with someone who seems to bring out your most unattractive traits. It is a challenge to stay in that loving place when you are looking at him or her or whatever situation is present. In those moments, don't despair.

Gratefully acknowledge the gift they've given you. In these times of dwindling duality, you have no choice but to see who you are really are – live, in 3D. It's not pretty, yet it is an absolute treasure.

You are vibrating into a dimension of love. Not love for only a few chosen ones, or a few isolated parts – love for all. With your body, heart, mind and soul you are moving on. In order to do so, all parts of you have to agree. Every component of your wonderful self has to say "yes". You can't partially ascend – It's all or nothing. Your individual capacity for self-love will determine just how this goes for you. Agape is your insurance policy.

You are here to love the world as she moves to a place that vibrates differently – rapidly and beautifully. You can best assist when you do the same yourself.

Honor the One that is you. As you are a component of the One that is us, this is all you need do. Care for yourself. Do not dismiss a negative emotion. Look at it squarely and thank it, it is an arrow directing you to a new facet of yourself to love.

This is your task now and it is no small one. It is perhaps the most important thing you'll ever do. Completely, selfishly, lavishly and in no uncertain terms love yourself. As you do, all of us feel it and are raised up. You are helping transform a world. It is the only thing left to do.

Once you see only gifts to love rather than problems to solve, your whole world becomes one big party. It's being held in your honor. We are so happy you've finally arrived.

You are the one we've been waiting for.

See you tomorrow.

Day 4*

I plan to explore today what oneness *isn't*.

Duality is screaming to get your attention. Who are you? Are you someone who hates? Are you someone who loves? Do you buy all this love and light jazz or are you convinced it is the physical you that is real? You are being asked to choose.

Believing in the love that you are is the ultimate statement of truth, of faith. Whatever is showing up for you right now – debt, fear, illness, anger, hatred or loss of any kind is merely a test. It cannot be ignored, and it is multiple choice. It is not pass/fail; there are many ways to complete it successfully. Within you is the right answer, the one that suits your heart. You know what to do. You came for this. Remember.

Your spiritual evolution will continue in the most perfect fashion, following whichever blueprint you construct right now. It is my deepest belief that tells me you are love. We are not different from each other after all, and you would understand.

It is faith that will see you through. Faith in love or light or God or Source or whatever term you use. Faith in something beyond what your eyes are seeing. *You are not your body. You are not your stuff. You are divinity; an intricate piece of the fabric of life, woven into oneness.* You have done more than read these words today; you have possibly saved a soul. As you turn on and shine your own light, you illuminate those within your world and there is no telling how far this light now reaches.

For darkness is only eradicated with light; with you. Take care of your issues that show up today, completely and with a strong heart. Yet do not embody them. For they do not define you, love does.

You are so much more than you know.

Day 5

Today begins the second half of your Quest.

The path to Agape will take you to Oneness. Self-love is love of the One that you are. The One that you are is a piece of divinity. We are connected. You spring from Source, and you never let go. So, we are moving in a circle, finding our way home, returning to the beginning, which is One.

The path to Oneness is Agape. Do you see how this works? Absolute love for you yields Universal Unconditional Love. There are in fact no separators between you and all of us. Once you accept yourself completely, we all start to look a whole lot better.

It is not that you tolerate or overlook your perceived "faults", or ours. It's not that you would have made every choice in the same way that you did the first time, or the same way that we did. It's not that you even want to spend a great deal of time with every single one of us.

It's that you comprehend at a very deep level that we are alternate versions of you. *Loving you means, by definition, that you love the rest of us.*

It's that easy and that challenging. Our world is a hologram. The best science today doesn't know precisely how it works, yet quantum physics tells us that what's in your mind is projected out to become what's in your world. What you think about yourself is what you will see in everyone else.

Fill your head with love and what will happen to your life will astound you. Imagine a world filled with people who loved themselves. This is what you are here for; you are here now to create and then participate in that world.

You've been practicing for such a long time — trying out a little agape here and some unconditional love there. Never sure when the show was set to begin, you fell back often to self-hatred. There have been so many reasons. Your body, your job, your grades, your past, your performance, your "mistakes" and your relationships each offer plenty of opportunities for failure, disappointment, guilt and blame.

Well it's show time. You've had your dress rehearsal. You know your lines and you know how this story ends. This curtain will close on a myriad of wonderful depictions of unity. You've been singing songs of love and writing movies of success forever — now it's time to sing them in your everyday and watch them play out in your homes. You've been telling yourself your own story – you just never knew it was real.

It is real. Most of what we've been force fed is the lie. You have no enemies. God has no favorites. There are no mistakes. Judgment is an archaic idea that creates fear and diminishes your power. It is not possible to hold judgment while loving absolutely.

Your power resides in your love. This strength is yours right now. Call it forth. This light is what you are. Feel it rise up and watch the faces of your loved ones light up when you shine it upon them.

This is what you've come for; to love. Once you love yourself, the entire world is your Beloved.

We are One. One spark, here now to get this whole place lit up. Our light has been hidden beneath shame and sadness, fear and debt, servitude and low self-esteem. No one has been able to convince you of your greatness – until now.

You know now that to claim your perfection is not arrogance, but truth. You are components of the One; self-love is the key to Ascension.

It is an honor to share this time with you.

Day 6

This is a different sort of Quest. You are not heading out into unknown territory. You know exactly where this love is located. It was there when you started and it's still there right now. You are searching for that which you are. You are love.

How can it be that you've forgotten? How is it that you've lost the map? What has happened to your GPS (Global Positioning System)?

It's been tampered with, you've been distracted, and as a result most of us today distrust the internal sense we arrived with.

You were born fully cognizant of your wisdom. You understood the light that you were and knew where the switch was located. Your heart held the key. No one had to tell you that you were wonderful and yet they did, often.

The life of an infant in cradled in love. That infant makes no effort to find or get that love and yet, there it is. An infant, most recently from Source, knows absolutely nothing of society. It is cared for and loved without condition every day. It is held, fed and showered with all good things – giving nothing in return.

"Ahhhh", you say, "but babies are irresistible, they are beautiful, precious miracles – What's not to love?"

"Indeed", would be my reply, "as are you."

A baby is an agape machine. It sleeps when it is tired, eats when it is fed and loves without holding back. It is born brilliant. Have you ever been present at the birth of a child? There is a light, a force that is emitted from both child and mother. It is magic.

Babies emanate love until we adults teach them not to, and they stop using their own memory. They are born loving their fingers and their toes and their torso and their voice and their thoughts and their sexual organs. There is nothing they dislike about themselves. Their self-love sort of leaks out of them and we see it, falling in love with them again and again every day.

We call them angels and precious and miracles and beautiful. They do not protest; they are in full agreement. This is my deepest wish for all of us. That we find ourselves, all grown up now, in full agreement with these words:

> *"You are a miracle. Source had a unique and brilliant idea and here you are. You began with one precious thought – absolute unconditional love. You beamed gloriously forth*

to join us here; to illuminate us with the love of our creator."

You volunteered to lose your way; only as a method of education and advancement. The brilliance that you are can best be seen in contrast, and so there has been darkness.

It is time to turn on your vibrant light, to remember where the switch is located. I don't have it. It is not in your wallet. It is not in your closet. It is not in the words or actions of anyone else. It is in your very heart.

You need nothing to complete this journey. Who you are – is right here, whispering, waiting and oh so ready to be found.

Remember. A baby just lies there, loving itself and the whole world follows suit. It is time for you to do the same. You are a piece of perfection; there is nothing else you need. You are a brilliant being, a vibrant light. There is no way for you to be lost any longer. We've found you.

You are coming to the end of this journey and we can see your light now, guiding each of us home.

Thank you.

Day 7*

Hello. You arrive today at your beginning, the place where love was planted. It rests within you. It's always been there. You just had to turn the light on so you could find it.

Your light is on now. You may need to install fresh batteries now and again to keep it going. That's okay; you know where to get them and which ones work the best. They are found in the places that feed your heart.

You are a component of the One – an integral part, necessary and unique. In 1898, Konstantin Stanislavsky said "There are no small parts, just small actors". Sometimes you imagine your light unimportant or too tiny to make a difference.

Once I found myself sort of stuck in the corner of a tightly packed storage facility. Half of our stuff was packed there as work was being done on the house. It had taken longer than anticipated, and because the children wanted their beloved decorations for an upcoming holiday, I was searching through stacked to the ceiling boxes, piled all around me. Then the power went out, and all went black.

For a moment, I panicked. I was alone and not sure anyone even knew I was there. But I opened my cell phone and became illuminated. It was small, dim and didn't stay lit for more than ten seconds at a time, but it helped me find my way. Now it took a while and crawling around with my phone in my mouth left a few bruises, but I made it − thanks to that tiny light.

We are all like that. You just don't know how far your words reach, or the effect one generous thought can have. The really cool thing is, you don't have to. As you focus on loving yourself, your light expands as does your reach.

The light that you are is vital. Know that you are a microcosm of the whole. What is happening in your heart is being played out in our world. Love yourself. With the energy of your love and the power of your light you change everything. You came to discover just what you could do in such a dark place. You came to light the way.

You are so much more than you know. The brilliance of you is bringing us all to a place of unparalleled beauty. You were made for this.

We are in sort of crazy times. All around it looks like the power went out. Your light is so important now. Be that one-in-a-billion light source that changes everything. You know how.

Just love. Against all odds and in the face of every negative thought, word or situation — refuse to be afraid. You know who you are. You are a piece of the divine here to spark a passionate healing flame of Agape. This is not for the faint of heart. The strongest among us took this on. You are one of the light bringers, the ones who said "yes".

You are powerful, capable and oh so ready for this. It is an honor to witness. As you push your way out of the dark and emerge, brilliant and beautiful, our world is forever changed.

You are the One we were waiting for.

This completes your Quest. Thank you.

*Blasts from the Past

Prelude

This is the invite that was sent that month of August 2012.

"Our Quest will come at a time when we will need to connect. As we journey this month, we will begin to see what it is to walk in oneness. Oneness is felt when it is understood that you are love, living in love, surrounded by love, talking to love, looking at love. It is all you. It is all divine. We are perfection. As we deeply love ourselves, accept every inch of our bodies and hearts and souls, we naturally expand out to deeply love our world. The idea of self-love is only unusual when you believe you are separate from it all. We are not separate. We are one. This month, on this journey, we will gently tip toe into unity and we will bring our agape with us.

The Shift starts there. We cannot hope to move from polarity to unity with judgment and blame filling our minds. We cannot move forward with fear. It is love that will create this Shift. Our goal is agape. We are One.

For love is always true. What may be confusing us is our definition of love. Love needs no definition. Love is what you are.

See you on the Quest."

Day 1

"I was recently asked, "What is a Love Quest?" Those of us who have been here since they began (a year and a half ago) will remember that we started by loving ourselves in our bathroom mirrors. These Quests are the ultimate journey to truth, the path to Ascension. Ascension is a rising up to a faster vibration. The hallmark of this place we are moving to is love. We are not truly going anywhere. We are becoming that which we are. We are love."

Day 2

"I am surrounded in vibration; the high school drum line is rehearsing. A combination of different sizes, shapes and sounds all composed of three identical things – a teenage boy or girl, a stick and a drum. Each sound unique yet together, when they pull it off, One rhythm. It is powerful and runs right through you; you can feel it as One sound.

Oneness is like that. Seven+ billion elements contribute to our One Verse. If our perspective was different and we could step back, wwwaaaaaayyyyyyy back, we'd hear the note we were singing.

Yet we are not back far enough and so we must rely on our internal senses to guide us as we sing; we are singing a love song."

Day 4

"I think that it is easy to talk virtually about love and light and unity and then blame your boss or carry anger for what your ex-lover "did". In perfect synchronicity, my everyday life has been swimming in duality. Actually, if it wasn't for this Quest, I'd be drowning. This has turned out to be more than I bargained for. In no uncertain terms, I am dealing with duality.

These Quests began in the Spring of 2011 and were never intended to continue past the first one. It was suggested as a way to explore in "real time" with each other what it means to love yourself. I was a different woman then and walked around with a large wad of blame in my pocket. After the first Quest, we all wanted more and here we are today, with monthly journeys and no end in sight. The fact that Face Book shut down the first account hardly seems to matter. Love prevails.

But what is not love? It seems to be cropping up everywhere I look this week. The whole notion of "what you believe is what you create" makes little sense if you are thinking about illness and poverty and physical harm. Yet, the law of attraction exists.

So, what's the deal? Today I find myself dealing with issues of health and money and watching highly evolved people whom I love deeply doing the same. It all comes down to self-loathing.

It has to stop. We've all probably watched "The Secret" and "What the Bleep" and read Neale Donald Walsch and Abraham Hicks and heard Mike Dooley and many other teachers. We actually do know how this works. We've been inundated with educators because the programming runs so deep. We've learned well, it is the un-learning that will set us free.

There are two thoughts that separate and isolate us. One is that we are somehow "different". Two is that "No one would understand". Both are false. A few years back I attended a seminar and the scariest part was this: you stood up and told the group, 100+ people, the worst secret you could muster up about yourself. I was terrified. As I listened and then took my turn I realized that appearances reveal nothing and second of all my worst was pretty much status quo. We've all been there. We've all done "worse" and we all deserve love in spite of it."

Day 7

"This Quest has had a deeper significance for me. A very close love of mine is about to undergo surgery. He is a veteran and

came home 7 years ago with more in his body than he left with. If you'd just send your light to my hero, specifically tomorrow, it would help. Namaste.'"

Oneness

Prelude*

This week, we will look a bit further.

Each day, for 7 days, look into your mirror.

Say "I love you."

Say "I accept you as you show up."

Say "I accept all versions of you that show up as someone else today."

Say "There are no versions I refuse to love."

Say "This feels amazing."

Smile now. It is going to be all right.

Have an amazing week of unexpected agape.

Welcome. Please follow along one day at a time.

This is not a race. Everyone wins on the Love Quest.

Day 1

You are in a fast moving, spectacular time in your life and in the life of your planet. With each passing day, you become more aware of our unity. We are inextricably entangled, creating and experiencing the results of our work simultaneously. As time speeds up, it becomes more and more challenging to separate out where things start and where they end.

You are on this Quest to explore Agape. Unconditional self-love takes on a much larger scope when Oneness is part of your self-definition. We are indeed the same stuff. This week will be about what that looks like in your every day.

Quantum physicists speak of entanglement. *Entanglement IS the dream.* We are walking and talking, loving and living in a mutually agreed upon reality. I exist on a back drop of what you believe you see around me. I most likely agree with your perception.

As you wake up, your consciousness expands to include other beings, dimensions, truths and possibilities. You see things you never noticed before. You are gradually realizing your world works much differently than you were taught.

We are One. What does that mean? It means that in some intricate and beautiful way, we are connected. To illustrate, imagine being on the other end of my stick, sort of like a see-saw. When I sit down, you can't help but be affected. You feel my reaction, and immediately I feel yours – up, down, up, down. In the same sense, you sense my pain, my joy, my love and my anger. You have to. This is how life works. We are One organism, opposite ends of the same stick.

We are becoming aware now of the power we hold. It has been deliberately manipulated so that we'd compete with and fight and fear each other. We are not each other's enemy. We are connected, very literally. To perpetrate anger at another being only intensifies pain, illness, war and hatred in your own life. The results of each are internalized in all of us. No one escapes. We are One.

When you look in the mirror today, with gentle smiling eyes, say hello to the world. Love who you see standing there. He is a child of God. She is walking divinity.

As you inch towards Agape, you will alter your world. That smile and gentle encouragement is felt by every bit of life in existence. You have access now to this truth. With help from many places and races, our minds and hearts are opening up.

As we individually love, it all changes. Generosity and compassion become the order of the day. Empowerment insists on it.

Love yourself and we will be blessed exponentially.

We are the Ones we've been waiting for.

See you tomorrow.

Day 2

Welcome to your second day.

With a full heart for all the love found here, let's begin.

It is not true, not ever, that you are alone. Now, you may feel alone and look lonely, yet this is part of the illusion. The illusion of separation has been so powerfully magnified, that you have even imagined isolation. If only you could step way back and see the magnificent being that is you, surrounded by the rest of us, you would know for certain this could never be true. We are One.

You've been given this body, these eyes and heart to explore in tangible, physical ways what it is to love. To love in human form is an honor. Not every being has had this opportunity. You do. The physical world you inhabit is exquisite. Your eyes behold each finger, toe and body part, while sensing each gentle breeze, hot shower and passionate embrace. Your nose smells home cooked food today and memories fill your mind of another time and meal. Your senses are inundated 24/7 while your heart beats out "Love-Love-Love-Love".

To make sense of it all is a challenge. You look on the scale and see a few more pounds or hear your mate or child or parent complain and you imagine yourself imperfect. This is illusion and deep within you sense the truth. All the while, your heart is beating "Love-Love-Love-Love".

The din of society, government, anguish and fear threatens to drown out the truth of your heart. Your heart will not be silenced. As long as you are here in the physical, it will continue, synchronized with mine and everyone else's; "Love-Love-Love-Love".

To love is a privilege. One such as you only comes around once. There is no other who walks in your shoes. Only you understand what resides in your heart and then propels your life. This is good news. It means, my fellow human, that there is no one who is better equipped to love you than yourself. For regardless of relationship, you will always be the closest friend you have. Love yourself.

Be careful and tender; listen and allow. There is a reason for every emotion, thought, word and deed. You would not waste your time here in fruitless pursuits. You are a component of divinity, an integral part of the fabric of humanity. We are not complete without your particular thread.

Be patient with yourself. Treat yourself as you would an honored guest – you are. Here now to help us all, you have arrived right on time and with all you need. Trust yourself, love yourself and be yourself. You are uniquely suited to do so.

I am thrilled to take this Quest with One such as you. Thank you for showing the way.

See you tomorrow.

Day 3

As you begin your third day, it becomes important that you look at all of the relationships currently in your life; your physical, daily life contacts. You do not exist in isolation. Even if you live alone, you have a mail carrier, a grocer and a landlord. You have a job and work mates, maybe a pet. Each of these counts.

It is never true that you can see yourself as One with some of us, but not with others of us. One is a singular mindset. It blows out of the water words like superior, prejudice, privileged, bigotry and segregation. This is not to say those thoughts don't exist, they do, yet in the face of One, they become illusion.

Can I declare with a straight face that one finger is better than another? Better in what way? All are necessary to the function of the hand. I will admit that my ring finger surpasses my thumb when it comes to wearing certain jewelry, yet I would mourn equally the loss of either.

We are here for different purposes. We have incarnated to evolve and we have a ticket on the fast train to enlightenment. Our beginnings and paths differ, but not our goal.

So, what does Oneness look like in a sea of faces and bodies and nations and religions? It looks like love. It means no one is dismissed as irrelevant; old or young, patriot or anarchist, Muslim or Jew, gay or straight, black or white, yellow or red, Republican or Democrat, off-world or on-world. "Ohana means family. Family means nobody gets left behind. Or forgotten." (Lilo & Stitch, 2002)

As we contemplate Oneness, start at home. We are One. All of us, together, speak a singular voice. When you hear someone that irritates, frustrates, offends or annoys you, resist the urge to correct or ignore or dismiss. Breathe. It's all you and all okay. These are not lesser versions of Oneness, and they are not wrong, they are merely alternate expressions of humanity; each of them divine.

We are One unique fabric called Man. Our richness and texture are expressed in our diversity. We are 7 billion+ threads – woven together with a Master's touch. Relish the One that we are. You can see it everywhere, your mirror, your family, your street, your town, and our world.

Start local, real local. Appreciate each component of you, and then move out to your community. "Nobody gets left behind. Or forgotten"

Without any condition at all, I love you. You are the physical manifestation of One's thought; a perfect intention, every detail a miracle. Your light illuminates our home; this planet is a beacon of love. See your reflection everywhere you look, *it is* – and you are gorgeous.

See you tomorrow.

Day 4

Hello.

Today marks the halfway moment on this Quest. You are "Just as far in as you'll ever be out." (Anna Nalick — Breathe)

What does that mean? It means you have a choice. Right now. You can still go either direction, and with equal effort get where you are headed. You know what going back to duality looks like. What will it take to get to Oneness?

To proceed from here on you must be willing to see through the illusion. We have a saying in our house, you have to "buy the rubber suit"; a reference to the old Godzilla movies, where you could actually pick out the zipper on the monster. If you wanted to get the most out of the film, you had to ignore the zipper, and believe the costume.

For you to reach a state of unity you'll have to remember, with or without a zipper, that this is all a finely tuned performance.

I am not my body. I chose her to express and experience a lifetime. She's been here a few years, has a history and a future. Yet she is not me. I am a light, a force, a unique aspect of Divinity. I chose every moment she experienced. None of those moments define who I am. they were merely scenes in the play of my life. This is the truth for you as well.

In order for you to embrace Oneness, you must remember there is a rubber suit and notice always the light beneath. Life demands that you play your role – you are in costume. You look like fathers, mothers, sisters, brothers or orphans. You are privileged and poor, suffering and celebrating, vibrant and ill. You are doctors, lawyers, therapists, plumbers, engineers, scientists, musicians and teachers. This time, in this life, you have picked one, two or a dozen of these outfits to wear; these "rubber suits".

There is a difference between pity and compassion. Have compassion without pity, for pity separates and compassion unites. In this life you may appear to be more fortunate than some others. If that is true, and you are moved to share your abundance, then do so. Always give in a way that honors the recipient without creating a state of being beholden or subservient. The roles you choose are many. Rest assured you have at one time walked in everyone's shoes, as they have in yours.

Without these shoes we are One. There is no difference – we've all come to serve. What are we serving? We are propelling our own evolution – individually and collectively, by playing out our roles. We are serving the ultimate gift — we are offering love. It is what emanates from our very pores and right through these shoes and rubber suits.

When you engage with another who appears to be in need, you have been gifted. He or she is shining a light on a part of you that you need to see — whether it be compassion or indifference; their presence has called it forth. There is no right or wrong, there is only experience.

From here on, in order to proceed towards Oneness, you'll have to remember the "rubber suit" and honor the light within. Every time.

If you can get there, as often as possible, your travelling will be easy. Then Oneness will be all that you see, and your path will be brilliantly lit with the lights of our seven billion+ hearts.

We are the One we've been waiting for.

Thank you. It is an honor to be here.

Day 5

Today you are on the second half of your Quest for Agape. As we proceed, we'll encounter lots of "Stitch's". In the movie, "Lilo and Stitch", Lilo was consistent about one thing – love. The object of her affection was a destructive, mono-syllabic weird looking alien. There was nothing warm and fuzzy about this pet. Lilo decides he's family and will not leave him behind; an extreme example of unconditional love.

Lilo could not know the motivation of Stitch, yet she identified with him as another lost soul, lashing out at a world he didn't understand and that couldn't understand him.

We are all Stitch to some degree. There are no exceptions. We are here for reasons we don't fully recall, trying to fit in, do the right thing, find some love and happiness.

You came to this life because you wanted this incredible opportunity. You are going to experience in one lifetime both extremes – polarity and unity. You will advance while physical, and the intensity of that experience is what you came for. Comparatively few beings signed on for this – being human is hard. Yet you did, confident you could pull it off. A shift of such magnitude that it's been heralded "The Shift of the Ages". This is what you agreed to conduct. You are not watching this happen, you are making it happen.

In the home stretch now, you are looking around wondering how you'll ever cross the finish line. You may also be contemplating what the prize is.

First – the how – *without judgment.* Every circumstance, each mistake, every outburst or criticism or atrocity witnessed you'll view without blame, accusation or fault finding. There is a difference between seeing clearly the person responsible for an action and hating him or her for it.

The first demands clarity of vision while the second incorporates duality. Agape does not mean that suddenly all behavior is allowed to go on and that it is okay with you. In a world such as ours, which has been deeply enslaved in density and polarity, the complete change to "service to others" will take a while. Many here will remain in the "service to self" modality for a bit. Our challenge is what to do when they impact our life.

First, love. All are equal here. We are One. Hatred and punishment are not necessary, while removal and re-education most definitely apply.

In our personal relationships, the option for re-education may not be there, yet we can always step away. "Service to Others" does not mean *without* service to you, *it includes you. You are all others; they are mere reflections of the One that you are.*

This is where your Quest began and where it must go. Love that man or woman in the mirror. All actions, thoughts, and words support her; everything he does begins with acceptance. You are okay. You are more than okay, you are a champion.

The prize is bliss. Absolute joy ensues when you see only love. Regardless of what your focus is, you are witnessing the workings of God. This is possible with agape. Loving the One that you are yields astonishing happiness. No longer are you wasting your moments in judgment or pain. You will stand in the truth of your divinity and establish a firm ground of love. All who enter will be encased in the radiance of Agape. No mistakes. No exceptions. This is where you are headed. It is what you came for. This prize cannot be measured in terms of earthly wealth, it is priceless.

I love you so very much.

See you tomorrow.

Day 6

Love is a truth. You can throw things at it, yell at it, call it names, hide it, cover it, refuse to acknowledge it, deny it or ignore it; yet it will remain.

Love is the foundation of each interaction, every relationship and all of life. None of this would be here if not for love. You exist in a world of form; birthed from Agape. You are the outsourcing of God's love.

The acceptance of oneness is a gradual process. As you look into your own eyes and find your inner light, you simultaneously discover the light in each other. We are ever seeking beings, pushing forward always for more. Expansion and growth are the methods of our evolution. As you begin to love truly the One that is you, you naturally notice the love that is me. Love is not an end, it is the beginning. There is no end to Agape, for the One that you are is infinite.

Love yourself and set free the bonds of ownership and duty that bind your relationships. Love cannot be owned and it is not exclusive. It is a force.

Love is a fierce knowing of truth; an acceptance of every dark and wonderful, passionate and violent, hideous and exquisite facet of life.

To experience Agape is a fearless act. There is nothing that cannot be said or done or looked at. It is acceptance without judgment. You are here because you are a fellow Master. If there is anyone who can pull off Agape in this controlled, violent, angry and divisive world — it is you. You were chosen to do this. You have all that is required.

This Quest is not for the faint of heart. This is the Ultimate Quest. Fearlessly look into the eyes of all life that is before you and love. Whatever it takes to unconditionally honor — give it willingly.

There is no loss in love. You have enough for me and the rest of us as well. Contrary to what you've been told, love multiplies as it is shared, *exponentially.*

If you just practice acceptance, open your eyes and see the love that surrounds you, you would be astounded. You think that it will take so much effort, when in fact your reward will be beyond description.

Agape is freedom; your gift to the world comes from your very own heart. See the One that you are and love yourself without reservation. It is a simple, yet revolutionary act.

You are the One we've been waiting for.

Thank you for being here. Tomorrow is the conclusion of this Quest.

Day 7

You are completing your Quest right now. Today is the last day of this journey and you can see your destination.

Although it's always been there, it may well have been invisible. Wrapped in blinders of should and judgments, you could not see Agape. It is obvious to you now. Clear vision is available to you always, yet it sometimes shows up in surprising ways.

"Hook" (2003) is a story of finding yourself again, after a long time of loss. Peter Pan has forgotten how to fly. What he needs is simple; he must find his happy thought. What is your happy thought?

From Agape flows a constant stream of smiles. The point of this Quest was to find an eternal source of love. It has been here always, right there in your heart.

Love yourself. Robin Williams took on a persona that was not his true nature; he left Never Land to become a Pirate. It took the smallest of the Lost Boys to see the truth; Peter Pan was still there, only hiding.

What it took for Peter is a moment of decision; he had to first realize he had lost himself, and then admit he needed help to find the way back. He had to ask. This is the moment you must create. By joining this Quest, you made a choice to look for Love. Will you recognize it when it shows up? This is who you are.

What is your happy thought? Find it, tuck it carefully in your pocket and repeat it relentlessly. It must run right through you to work — its power resides in its truth. You must not only believe that it's true, you must know it.

Know who you are. It is love that sources your power and will lift your wings in flight. Neverland or the Next Dimension or just plain happiness; it is found right here. You made it.

A constant stream of "Yes." will assure you never get lost again.

Read your happy thought over and over until it remains a part of you. It is. You are meant to fly. Agape means it's all okay. You are right on time and we are thrilled you found your way back.

This is who you are. A force such as yours could not be denied. The light that is you is brilliant. We are only too happy to bask in your glow. We've been expecting you.

You are the One we've been waiting for.

*Blasts from the Past

Prelude

Here is the invitation, as it went out in September of 2012:

"Our September Quest will come at an intense time for all of us. Having begun to see ourselves as One, we will be recognizing how it came to be that we have imagined our separateness. As we learn the truth, it will be tempting to turn around, and focus on the untruths, and those behind them.

In this Quest we will make a stand for the One that we are. No longer will we see ourselves as separate. No longer will we love just some of us/ourselves, and hate some of us/ourselves, praise some of us/ourselves and blame some of us/ourselves. We are One.

We will look this month into our own eyes and recognize our greatness and our perfection; our light will become visible. Our imagined "faults" and those of our brothers and sisters are no longer the point. Love is the point. It is time for you to shine. The Shift starts there. We cannot hope to move from polarity to unity with judgment and blame filling our minds. We cannot move forward with fear. It is love that will create this Shift. Our goal is agape. We are One.

For love is always true. What may be confusing us is our

definition of love. Love needs no definition. Love is what you are.

See you on the Quest."

Prelude*

> As you awaken this morning, prepare to begin your Quest by throwing back the covers.
>
> What you'll notice there, beneath the layers, is you.
>
> Meet yourself in the mirror, each morning for a week.
>
> Really look, until you find yourself.
>
> Say "It's okay. I know all the places you've been hiding."
>
> Say "You can come out now. I will not reject you."
>
> Say "I want to know you."
>
> Say "Show me who you are."
>
> Say "I will show you the same."
>
> Now spend this week, discovering the wonder that is you.

Welcome. Please follow along one day at a time.

This is not a race. Everyone wins on the Love Quest.

Day 1

Welcome to your Love Quest.

It's time to decide. Agape is a fearless act. Are you up for it?

It demands honesty, bravery and belief. In order to love yourself you must first be aware of whom it is you are loving. The blindfolds are off, the shields are down; ego does not need protection from agape. What you need is acceptance. The only word is "yes"; it answers every protest.

"Can I love myself knowing all I've done?" "Can I love myself even when I'm angry?" "Can I love myself after I screwed up?" "Can I love all of my human faults?" "Can I trust myself?" "Can I fearlessly scrutinize my body and love all my parts?" "Can I let go of self-blame?" "Can I stop all this judgment?" "Really?"

On the face of it, love seems an easy choice. Would you rather be contented and uplifted or frustrated and miserable? Within you is where your happiness springs, and where the only thing that'll lift you up permanently is found.

Love is not originated "out there". Love does not begin anywhere but your own heart. Your loves are reflections of your deepest beliefs about you. Although intellectually the choice is an easy one, our childlike tendency to be thrilled with ourselves has been eroded. Our elders and our society have each taught us guilt and judgment and we've learned well. This is not truth.

We are on a Quest for truth and it must be taken alone. No one but you know the depths of your self-loathing or the images that you fear. It is time now to see clearly. These ideas have not served you.

You are beginning to see the manipulation and control that was your life. As facts are uncovered and plans are exposed, you become empowered. We've been lied to by every institution we believed in; religion, government, financial, health and education.

The time now is not for blame or regret. It is time to rebuild; the moment to love has arrived. Unconditional and fearless agape is what will empower us to demand truth and transparency from each other. For we are worth it.

One such as you is a gift to all of mankind. Your arrival was planned and celebrated by all of creation. This moment now is about the realization of your worth; the acceptance of your divinity. We are One. Source, God, Creator or whatever term works for you – had a brilliant plan. The success of that plan depends on you. Your part is simply told – you are here to love fearlessly. In doing so, the realization of Oneness is achieved; you will walk in Paradise.

It is an honor to walk by your side. Your Quest continues for 6 more days, thank you for showing up.

We've been expecting you.

You are the One we've been waiting for.

Much love.

Day 2

Hello. Today you'll continue with your Quest.

First, a story, a personal one.

What's been going on for me is that I took the words from yesterday and absorbed them into every fiber of my being. A sort of battle ensued.

I am not sure what instigated it, but it was no longer possible to be partially or half way in – I was either in or out. It became time to walk my talk – it was Agape or continued self-loathing. I had to make a choice.

This was not a choice that could be made on social media. This choice had to spring from my heart and from my soul. It was not easily made and not pretty to watch.

It began with nothing to say, and then proceeded along with a litany of reasons to despise who I was. I gradually began to speak. I believe my body had a decision to make. The love from everyone here brought me to a choice point. Was I love or was I a 'poser?

I gave up for a day or so – there was no light. Perhaps you'd call this my Dark Night of the Soul. It felt that way. I've had one before, many years ago. I didn't know you could have more than one.

A whole host of reasons and lovers and words later, I began to feel like love again. It is different now. It feels real. I am not a 'poser. I am love.

I don't know if my words sound different to you today, but they do to me. Although I have always believed them and known them – *now I am them.*

There is no outside force that will alter this truth. I know who I am. We have journeyed together on these Quests through forgiveness to Agape, and we are headed for Oneness. We can help each other with encouraging words, pictures and videos as we continue. Yet the real knowing is not found in any of those places.

You will know you've found love when no one can cause you to doubt it. **They can yell at you, leave you, fire you, steal from you or hurt you – yet they cannot remove from you your truth.**

You cannot hate them or blame them. You do not hate or blame yourself. You are divinity in shoes, a spark shot forth from Source, light in a human suit. You are love. So is everyone else.

You are here to demonstrate that One Truth. Self-love is the foundation of your brilliance. No one knows better than you the strength of your soul. Show us your beauty and gift us with your wisdom. *You are the One we've been waiting for.*

With deepest gratitude and overwhelming love.

I will see you tomorrow.

Day 3*

Welcome to your third day.

Oneness is a singular decision. It is truth, yet today you are realizing how your beliefs and societal structures have held it to be fantasy. It takes commitment and tenacity to work at understanding this; oneness is a foreign concept. In order to change your belief systems, you must first accept the possibility of unity.

Unity demands clear vision and unconditional acceptance of yourself. Only with blinders off can you love absolutely. You, who know every inch of yourself, are not here to judge that which you know. You, who are unlimited consciousness, are here to love your limited physical self. It is only through the realization of your infinite divinity that you can see clearly. This is what this journey is about — you are on a Quest for the Truth.

The love that you are is the purest force you command. It is the core of your power; the center of life. This is how your world is created, it springs from intent. See through every false image to your deepest truth. Intend only love.

For love is your starting point, your finish line and every inch in between. There is nothing but love in your blueprint. You cannot escape love, it is your foundation. Anything else is mere decoration, pretty, but only on the surface.

Agape is deep self-acceptance. This Quest takes you beyond your human trappings, into the raw center of your soul. We are One – a force of unprecedented power. This moment on your journey asks you only to love.

It is the most challenging, yet simplest request. Do you love yourself? Do you love me? How about everyone else? Do you love yourself without reservation or hesitation?

Say yes. Choose love. You are a beautiful, powerful, joyful light being, here to discover your brilliance. Your light is so very much needed now. It is no accident you are reading these words, *for they are written for you.*

With a full heart, take your love and visualize it spreading from your head to your toes and back again. Feel the beauty of who you are. Imagine all of us feeling the same. This wave of agape will heal us all. We are One, we are Love and we are so ready to do this.

Just love. You are the One you've been waiting for.

See you tomorrow.

Day 4

This is your fourth Quest day.

It's been a different journey, interrupted and intensely personal. A good thing, for that is more like life, a series of interruptions into a very personal string of moments. Perhaps, on this Quest, you'll go places you haven't before, off the beaten track.

You are looking for Agape. What has to be decided here? It isn't whether or not you *WANT* to love yourself; you wouldn't be here if you didn't. It's not whether or not you *CAN* love; each one of us is capable. You were born with the ability to love. What you are deciding is whether or not you *WILL*. It's a choice you will make privately.

Agape has always been here, hiding in plain sight. You began these Quests because you didn't know. It seemed your world, your life, was chock full of reasons and people and situations that were making you miserable. You were never told to love yourself. It seemed the world was out to get you.

Love came quietly and crept at first in through our bathroom mirrors. We forgave the only one we could. By looking into our own eyes and searching for some gentleness, we began to see the truth. It starts with you.

There is only one who can complete this journey; only you know which path to take. Your inner voice whispers; only you can hear your own protests. Just as you arrived with a heart full of unique gifts, you've carried your own sack of guilt and another of NO. These you are looking to leave behind. They are weighing you down and preventing you from succeeding.

For anything that does not feel like love – is fear. Fear wears many disguises. There are some really good ones, let's look at some of the best – *disappointment, sadness, remorse, guilt, anger, blame, judgment, frustration, impatience, intolerance, rage, hate, subservience, worship (rather than honor), obedience (rather than cooperation), hate, cruelty, low self-esteem, worry, dissatisfaction, expectation (could be high or low), requirements, conditions, self-loathing, disgust, ridicule...* Each of these hides fear. Beneath these masks you'll find the same thing, every time. If you add mutual respect to any of these commonly used phrases, they become a different thing altogether. It takes courage to remove them.

You may have heard that FEAR is an acronym in English for "False Evidence Appearing Real". Well, if you take it a step further you can see that all around you is illusion, *until you see through eyes of Agape.* You are not this body – you are love. All fear, regardless of which mask is covering it, is fear of loss. As an infinite spark of divinity, *there is nothing you are capable of losing. All that you are is love.*

This human suit with your current mask is a vehicle. Its purpose is to get you someplace. You are headed for Truth. You'll find it by removing your mask and then seeing what it is you are afraid of. Once you do, let it go.

There is nothing to lose in Agape. Life without the mask is weird, but only for a moment. You see, the words you've been whispering have not been heard by us. They have been for your ears only. Our ears are saturated with our own reasons for our own masks. We look at you and see only love. The mask you wear is only visible in your own mirror.

Remove the mask and what you'll find is you. He is brave and brilliant, she is beautiful and gentle. You are One. The fear you've been protecting with your mask isn't real. Only love is real.

Do something fearless. Look into that mirror with eyes of Agape. You are perfection. There is nothing to hide. There is only that which you are beneath the mask. You are love. It is your truth that propels us all.

I am so glad you have joined us.

You are the One we've been waiting for.

Day 5

It is your fifth day.

Realize that your image of yourself is distorted, along with your image of everyone else. There are a few among us who see clearly – they are the avatars, prophets, and holy ones, as well as some regular folks. They will emit mostly peace and with them you'll feel only serenity. In their eyes will be love.

They can be found behind cash registers, in shoe stores, in temples and on the street. It is not their title, moniker or clothing that identifies them – it is their essence. They embody agape. When you are held within their gaze, unconditional acceptance is all that you feel.

This is your destiny – the ending place that then becomes your beginning. With open love filled eyes your life looks radically altered. You behold yourself in the morning mirror and grin – today begins another adventure. Where will love lead you? It is the path your heart lays out for you that becomes the Quest for Agape. Regardless of occupation, you are working for only one thing, heading towards one truth. All paths take you home.

You and I are consciousness, expressed in physical form. The efforts to convince us otherwise have not worked – we have woken up. We are conscious now. We know who we are.

With that awareness we can no longer be misled or unloved or enslaved. Consciousness is love – Source is Agape. This is the fabric of your being. You are not just a race or a job or a sex or a body or a name or any other physical attribute. You are One. An expression of divinity is evidenced in your every moment. You are worthy. There are none lesser or greater – You are One.

When you finally appreciate your sacred self, you will tenderly handle each other. It becomes not only a question of "what serves me" but "what serves us"?

We are One. By coming together here and in our physical life, we'll demonstrate how powerful we actually are. We are changing the future; you have already changed your past and we together are altering our entire world. It is you. All the love and wisdom capable of being stored in one place resides within. You only need to open up and recognize it.

Look past all "False Evidence" and be witness to the miracle that is you. You are here now to usher in a force of love never before seen on the planet. This is why you came and what has drawn

you to these words and on this Quest. Remember who you are —
you cannot help until you do.

You are love, pure and unblemished. You have come to transform
a world.

You are the One we've been waiting for.

Thanks for sharing yourself with us.

Day 6*

Hello again. It is your sixth day.

You are gathering yourself, collecting your strengths and fortifying your moments with love. This is as it should be. As you approach the end of this Quest, you can't help but feel the change.

This is where you are headed, to love without reason, to love as a constant stream, to love as often as you take a breath.

A quick personal story follows.

I participated in a training session a few days ago. There were five adults standing at computer terminals for several hours. The session was long and tedious. I was positioned between two people; one very quietly having a hard time and one very vocally doing the same. The quiet one sought no help while the vocal one wanted lots of it.

The other two adults stood next to each other and they formed a team. Thus, the training room was divided. In the half with the team there was laughter, collaboration and speed. In the other half there were sighs of exasperation with a great deal of anxiety, discussion and interruption. When I left, both adults in the "other half" were still at it and you could cut the tension with a knife.

The benefits of unity were crystal clear. The two who formed a team are now friends, while the other three don't know each other and had a long and painful afternoon. In all cases, the training was accomplished. How would you like to have participated, if given the choice? The team was made up of two unlikely cohorts, yet appearances made no difference. None of us knew each other before entering the room. The "rules" were for independent completion of the course; yet success demanded co-operation and "out of the box" thinking.

Agape and Oneness are not your usual way of getting through life. Things are not set up to make it easy for us. Society has been operating with another agenda. The operating principle has been "the end justifies the means". This no longer works. If you aren't yet approaching things that way, it will soon become obvious that in order to love, your focus has to be on each other and on collaboration.

You are not simply a means to an end. You are love. This notion demands a re-evaluation of all that you have learned. Life is no longer "business as usual". You are about at the finish line, you can see Agape just up ahead. It will take all of us, with our conflicting ideas, viewpoints, origins, handicaps and strengths, to get there successfully. The task is easily accomplished once we utilize the best tool we have — each other.

Remember this truth — you are not alone, you were never alone, and this singular journey of yours is being simultaneously taken by all of us as One. We are here to assist and to love. Everything else is merely background, the setting where we can join together and find agape in each other's eyes. This is why you are here.

We are the Ones *you've been waiting for.*

Thank you for your light.

Day 7

You've reached the final day of this Quest. It has been quite an adventure. Focused on making it real, this week did not disappoint. You've "weathered the storm" beautifully.

Congratulations. You have done it. You are moving from talking the talk to walking the talk – Agape is in your pocket. You realize now the truth of your divinity.

You may forget once in a while and that's okay, you are in new territory. It takes a while to completely understand this foreign landscape. Your internal GPS was only recently re-programmed. It's no longer about how long things take or how much things are "worth". The value is found in the doing, not just in the result. Your worth is found in your heart and held there always intact.

What does life look like through eyes of Agape? It looks like "Yes." You see co-operation, collaboration, unity and friendship. Your days expand in unsuspecting ways. The people in line for the cashier become opportunities to connect. You are never bored and always looking around for someone to smile at, offer a helping hand or listening ear to. Life is full.

Oh, you'll be tempted to ignore us but we are relentless. We are everywhere you go, gifting you with opportunities to love and experience oneness. This is a life of unity, a journey in the "next dimension". Your walls are down now; you've embraced us rather than shield yourself from us. Just watch what happens.

In this land of Agape, all is One. The old rules don't apply. Everyone is "out of the box". You've been getting ready for this your whole life. You're finally here. There is no one who knows better than you how much love you are capable of sharing – you are an infinite expression of agape.

The difference today is that you can see it; your eyes are open. You'll walk now with clarity and conviction. You are love. Agape is where you start. With every interaction and each conversation, every thought returns to this. There are no questions that you can't answer with love. Your method is uniquely suited to the specific spark of Source that is you.

YOU. *An amazing singular expression of all that is good.* Look into your beautiful eyes and smile, for there you see the eyes of Agape. Love, Love, Love yourself. There is none like you anywhere else.

You are the One we've been waiting for.

It has been an honor to journey with you.

*Blasts from the Past

Prelude

The Invitation for the October 2012 Quest follows:

"This is a Quest for Love. Self-Love. It starts with you and ends with me and organically becomes US. We are one.

This Quest comes at a time of choosing. We see played out in our neighborhoods and our world the extremes of unity and polarity. We are faced with a decision. How do we choose to proceed? What does it mean to be One?

In this Quest we will explore Oneness in a world that has been operating from a state of ownership, control and confusion - division. Agape demands fearless sight. In order to love the One that we are, we will have to peek under the covers and around the corners at every facet of ourselves. It is all divine.

We will look this month into our own eyes and recognize our greatness and our perfection; without reservation or condition. Our light is visible now. Our imagined "faults" and those of our brothers and sisters are no longer the point. Love is the point. It is time for you to shine.

The Shift starts there. We cannot hope to move from polarity to unity with exceptions. We cannot move forward with fear. It is love that will create this Shift. Our goal is agape. We are One.

For love is always true. What may be confusing us is our definition of love. Love needs no definition. Love is what you are. See you on the Quest."

Day 3

"The David Icke seminar, "Remember Who You Are" just ended. Some will find David hard to believe. He's been telling his story for two decades and it is being validated again and again today.

His message resonates because it does not back away from the hard stuff and concludes always with love. It is this conclusion we are looking to reach, as One."

Day 6

"As you approach the end of this Quest, you can't help but notice the timing. We have loved ourselves through a powerful storm. Hurricane Sandy calls on us to demonstrate our unity."

"As much of my family lives on the East Coast of the USA, I followed the events of the storm closely. There was a live feed from the town I was born in, so all day and night there were photos and reports. The stream was smattered with "Great job guys." and "Thank you." and "You guys are the best." along with pictures of groups of people helping each other out. All calls for

help were responded to, and from my point of view, it was as if one voice was coordinating it all.

That voice was Love. We are amazing. A crisis brings out the hero from deep within. The point of our Quest is to have that hero out all the time. "

Uncovering

Prelude*

This week will be like no other.

You will stand naked before the crowd in front of your mirror.

It is a crowd of one.

As you gaze at yourself each day, for 7 days, be sure to look beyond the layers.

Say "Hello there."

Say "What have you been hiding behind?"

Say "What are you still hiding from?"

Say "Is all this hiding worth your one precious life?"

Keep looking. Look deeply. You will find your answer. I promise.

Now in whatever way that works for you, remove your dark cloak of fear.

Toss it aside.

Now get dressed. We are waiting for you.

Welcome. Please follow along one day at a time.

This is not a race. Everyone wins on the Love Quest.

Day 1

Welcome to the beginning. You are here by choice. It is no accident you are reading these words. You've been hearing them whispered for so long now, just beyond audible. Maybe you'll recall them here.

What is it you are straining to hear? Truth. You'll know it when it arrives. For so very long now you've looked at oneness as if it has something to do with the other. Yet all is One. The "other" is not possible. It was always about you.

Oneness means there is nothing outside of you. Empathy and compassion are just the tip of the iceberg – they still focus outside of you. Oneness begins within. Full integration is where we are headed.

You must start by loving yourself. Then one day you'll realize there has never been anyone else.

You don't need fixing. You stand whole and perfect and you still are. You were born knowing you were flawless; a diamond in the rough. Around puberty, you forgot. It is then the sleeping began.

Prior Quests were the start of your awakening. Conscious now, you notice more. Contrast is everywhere – good, bad, happy, sad, blissful, angry, peace, conflict. That's why you stayed. You don't want to miss a thing.

You may still be drowsy. Some of us leap out of bed in the morning and some of us limp. In college I was awarded, more than once, the "bear in the morning" award. I guess you could say I'm a limper, not a leaper. Either way works. Eventually, full consciousness creeps in.

When it does, and when clear focus returns and you notice every "flaw", remember where beauty is found. It is found in the eyes of the beholder. Those eyes are yours. You are a mess of "imperfections". Look with wide open eyes and grin for each is your gift, leading you home. That's why you discovered them just now. Home is where you are headed. Home is in your heart and it is there the real treasure is found. It is there where agape waits.

You are the One you are waiting for.

See you tomorrow.

Day 2

You've moved further along on your Quest for Agape.

It is different than before. I know that you like things in nice, neat packages. You can wrap your head around them when they are presented that way. But this is not that sort of Quest. It ends in 6 days here, yet there is a depth and there are layers – each journey uncovers just a little bit more of each.

You cannot know the expansive and glorious intent of Source without an open and free heart. You must be willing to risk everything to discover the plan.

You are so much more than you know. This body, these jobs, your chores and life are just vehicles for exploration – they are not answers. Answers are found beyond them. You must be willing to step into discomfort. Once you are there, with every sense tingling, your eyes will open wide. Images, ideas, thoughts and feelings enter through every sensation – all of them new. Do not be afraid.

This is a journey of the heart, the most intelligent and powerful organ you have. It would not lead you astray. It knows where agape resides. It is found in you.

Dare to imagine yourself, naked and new before your eyes –
bathed in nothing but love. See every inch, know every thought,
remember every deed – and be. Just love. There is no place else
to look, no one to hide from, nothing to hide. It is you – just as
you decided to show up. Perfect.

The answers exist or there would be no questions. For you are
love – snippets of Source in human suits. "What you don't have,
you don't need." You know the solution before the problem is
given voice. Just listen. In the quiet you will find what you seek.
The wisdom, the teacher, the guide – is you.

The most extraordinary package remains unopened still. It holds
boundless love and looks like complete acceptance. Open it. You
are the one you are waiting for.

See you tomorrow.

Day 3

Welcome to the 3rd day on your Quest.

You are love in human form. There is deep resonance inherent in the idea that power does not need to be declared or granted, it merely is. By being so, it is then evident; recognized by everyone who is looking for it.

Yet we are a young race and have yet to experience freedom in physical form. We don't know what it looks like. We are on a learning curve.

When there is a place to go and it is a place that you have never been, it is a bit "nervousing" as my son used to say. You are unsure of the territory, the language, the culture. You may not have the answers right away; yet they exist. You are building a framework in which they can be expressed and translated, understood and enjoyed.

You have stepped now deeply into the truth of who you are.

You have held on to the idea that a new world exists and you have been looking for evidence of it. Perhaps you've expected its introduction to come from an off-world source, a God or a government. In fact – it has. As a sovereign being, you are all of the above. In order to know yourself capable of being your own keeper and holder of truth — you must be clear on who you are.

You are love — divinity on two legs. You've been leading yourself down this road for some time — one that holds no blame or judgment or other. This road to Agape is not just about feeling better. It is about being. It is an actualization of your truth. We are One.

Being all that you are demands first — awareness. Know yourself as love. Be the Creator God that you are. Stand in the fullness of truth and just BE. Be your wildest imaginings of yourself. Be free. As a being unencumbered with guilt, judgment or self-hatred — you will gift freedom to all you gaze upon. We are One.

The joy you feel when you are held in the clear gaze of a very young child deeply satisfies. Pure love does that. There is nothing else that holds value across time, space and dimensions; regardless of the market or amount. *Love cannot be quantified.*

Agape is pure love and you are born as an exquisitely wrapped package of it — a package of prosperity. Layers of shame and subservience cover yet do not diminish your worth. Nothing can. It is up to you to remember, to remove the layers and Be —

unafraid, unencumbered and free. You are a brilliant being of light here to demonstrate that truth.

See you tomorrow.

Day 4

It is your fourth day and you are right in the midst of your Quest. What can you do to guarantee success? You can love.

Agape is unknown territory. Solitary bliss without a mind-altering substance is not "normal". Agape, once discovered, offers accelerated joy, constant peace and a state of equilibrium. You cannot "rattle" a Master. All is happiness.

There is untapped potential within. You are a force. Access your power with love. Check out your smile, that unique stride you have, your laugh. Appreciate your sense of humor. Give yourself a hug.

As you do these things, and gradually accept your uniquely individual wonder – you'll find Oneness. You will be filled with wonder at the brilliance in each other. You will be "wonder – full".

We are each other's reflection. This world is illusion – a fun house at a carnival – a house of mirrors. Look around and you'll see evidence of what beliefs you are holding on to. What do you see?

As we re-birth this new age, this shifting consciousness, the walls, structures and institutions are crumbling. The belief systems you were taught turn out to be intentionally fraudulent. Conversation and contract are some form of manipulation. This has been your environment, your field of awareness, the backdrop of your reality.

It's neither good nor bad, it just was, it just is and it's in the process of changing. As it does, you discover it's all part of the same Quest you are on. You see, there are very few absolute truths and you are on this journey to find one of them. Once found, it cannot be lost; you carry it with you always. Agape is your very core.

You are an outsourcing of God, or whatever you call our Prime Creator. As drops of water are the Ocean, you also are Divine. Every attribute you hold has its origin in Eternal Essence, Love, God, Source. Every attribute you hold is sacred.

You must move into loving every part of yourself, as One, before you can move beyond. Beyond you'll discover love for every other, as One. It is from there you'll come to truth – there is no other – all is One.

You are transforming and your very language becomes a challenge. Names are separators and become unnecessary when you recognize alternate expressions of truth by their very essence rather than the name they've been given.

You are on a path to truth; Oneness. Agape sounds different than you expected it to; you've never lived here. Stay open, your heart is jubilant and itching to rejoice. You are a thought and can go anywhere.

Choose places of your deepest longing, without regard to should or can't. You are magnificent and full of wonder. Allow yourself to fly beyond restrictions of self-doubt. We are watching, learning and seeing ourselves in your flight. Thank you for being here and for sharing your journey.

Day 5

More than halfway now on your journey for acceptance, you face the obstacle that waits for us all – doubt. It exists in seven+ billion forms, each the same at their core – fear. What is your deepest fear? That you are not good enough. In some imagined way, you come up short.

Your aim is fearlessness. What would you do today if you were fearless? What would you wear? How would you prioritize? What would your answers be? How far would your imagination take you? Where would you go? For that is the life that awaits you.

As you proceed, and "get" that you are good enough, thoughts emerge. Thoughts of greatness, success, love, beauty, joy. These ideas feel good. That is the point. Nothing is more important than that you feel good. Your feelings tell you what it is you are in the midst of creating. They are your happiness signal; your success indicator.

Allow and encourage everything that brings a smile. Say yes. Guilt will fade away as you feel better, better, and better still.

There is this part in the movie "Hook" with Robin Williams as Peter Panning, talking to his son Jake. Jake is playing around and Robin says "Stop acting like a child." With his eyes twinkling, Jake smiles, laughs and replies "I AM a child." Act like a child before society taught you fear of reprisal. Just DO love.

Let this be your mantra. As a being of limitless potential – allow yourself to BE. DO what it is you came to DO – Love.

For there has been none before you and there will be none after that can love as you do. You've arrived now because your unique expression of divinity is necessary in our world. We need what you have – there is no one else who can supply it. Trust that small voice within. It is fearless. Know that you are loved. You are.

Without condition or exception, love yourself. This is how you are loved by Source; ridiculously, with wild abandon and without limit. Feel that love run through you and know that YOU are the one we've been waiting for.

See you tomorrow.

Day 6

This is a Quest for truth. Truth simply is. You are love. This you have heard many times. This Quest seeks understanding. You are looking to realize truth within. Agape is unconditional self-love. You are headed for love without requirement.

Using the word unconditional to further define love is sort of like using the word feline to further define cat. Love is unconditional. If your feelings change because conditions do, then what you thought was love – wasn't.

We love each other. Sometimes the connection of love is physical, sometimes it's emotional, sometimes it is mental and other times spiritual. It's not all or nothing; it may very well manifest as only one expression in this 3D life.

You may be wildly aroused by each other physically and have not much to talk about. That does not invalidate the love connection. You may share a deeply transformative spiritual moment with someone with whom you have nothing else in common. One or more than one expression of love connection can be present in any relationship, and none of them invalidate each other.

In a general sense, we all love each other. Love is what we are and what we do. In a specific sense, we choose our partners in business, romance and friendship according to where and how strongly that love connection is expressed. There is no quantifier for love; it is not more here and less there. It is merely expressed differently, and felt in varying degrees, places and ways. I love you. I do not love you less because I can't see you.

Heartache arises when we were hoping for absolute connection on all fronts and thought we'd found it. Relationships, with or without deep connections, are agreements. They begin, continue, and at some point, end. Both parties have to want to play.

Our Quest is about the most intimate relationship you'll ever have. This connection is guaranteed to be physical, emotional, mental and spiritual. When you awaken to the love of self, there are no disappointments. No unmet expectations. No surprises. No secrets. No change of heart.

Within you is the best friend you long for, the lover you dream of, the wise teacher you seek and the most fun playmate ever. Once you discover agape, you'll find deep satisfaction in all relationships. No longer will you be looking for them to be anything specific or to fill any unmet need – they can simply BE whatever it is they are. You will BE also – without judgment or requirement.

Freedom feels like this. Your Quest is for nothing less.

Your world will always be the physical expression of who we are within. No longer are we slaves to judgment and obedience and requirement and debt of any kind. We are realizing agape. There is no one who can take this journey for you. Yet, we are taking it as One.

Freedom is synonymous with love, regardless of expression. Your most jubilant moments have happened in utter abandon. This is where your Quest is headed. Once you arrive, your entire world will be about play. You will recognize joy as self-love and agape will be all that you see.

It promises to be exquisite and incredible and beyond what you've ever experienced. This is why you are here.

See you tomorrow.

Day 7

The love you are searching for is not actually lost. It is, like many other things have been, hidden. You'll have to understand what it is you are looking for, so that you will recognize it.

This love of self is indestructible. It cannot be dampened or diminished with falsehoods once it is realized. The holder of this love is reading these words. It does not come from another. It comes from you.

You arrived with agape. You spent hours observing and moving every toe and finger, marveling at their beauty. Your days were absorbed with discovering new ways to enjoy everything about yourself.

Your self-worth was fully intact. It took a planned and constant effort and a lifetime of manipulation to convince you that you were less than magnificent.

Agape is truth. It is not something that you do. It is that which you are.

You cannot see agape. It is what you know. Sometimes you look at a rock and it has a million-dollar price tag. Sometimes you look at a rock and it appears to be a cheap bit of coal. Yet both are diamonds, with the same core. We cannot see agape, it must be known.

Agape is not thinking "I look good today". It is knowing – "I AM good." There is no one better. Self-esteem is holding yourself in the highest esteem; looking up to yourself as a being of value, someone to emulate, someone to honor, someone to respect.

You have everything that is required. You have the components of miraculous. You are here because of your divine wonder, your sacred parts and the one of a kind gift that is you. If you don't remember yet what this means – ask. Deep within you'll find the answers. It is not that they don't exist. It is that you were never told.

It is time for you to know – you have come to show the way. Trust that you will remember. You have all that you will ever need. You are here because there is none other who can supply what you have. You have arrived with a heart full of agape.

Yet, like discovering a twenty in the pocket of an old pair of jeans, it was useless until it was once again found. Your Quest has discovered your agape. It is up to you to decide how to use it.

Remember your joy and wonder at even your most basic components – your fingers and toes. It is that fascination we return to with agape. You are unique, magnificent beings in marvelous bodies that think and speak and move and sing and dance. Allow yourself to be amazed — for Source is eternally entertained, fascinated and thrilled by your every moment.

Open the gift of agape. Remember to love without inhibition. Return to unrestrained enthusiasm about life. You are here.

You are meant to live in bliss and with agape remembered, you will. It is an honor to share this moment with you. Thank you for taking this journey.

It is now complete.

You are the one you've been waiting for.

*Blasts from the Past

Prelude

Here are some notes in preparation for this Quest. This one was held in January of 2013. It had been several months since the last one took place.

"In this Quest we will be One. Agape is a fearless act of courage. In order to love the One that we are, we will have to let go of every protest and absorb every facet of ourselves. This is it. The preparations have been completed. Who you are is perfect, as is. There is nothing else for you to do, it is time now to be. Just be love.

Look into your own eyes and witness divine love. Look into our eyes and see the reflection of divine brilliance. Your light is visible now. Nothing else can be seen; there is only truth. Without reservation or exception, shamelessly love us all."

"You reside in a field of love. Your very base programming begins there. It is the spark of each other that joins you. Isolated, you may appreciate nature and love life, yet it is in human contact that you embody the fierce power

of agape. For when you love another, it is not their attributes that are calling to your soul, but a reminder of your own.

When you look at each other and are deeply moved, it is because at a fundamental level you understand that there you behold the sacred. It is you that has stirred your own soul.

What this moment is about is a shedding of our skin of self-loathing"

I AM

Prelude

This week you will move your gaze down a bit.

As you meet yourself in the mirror, each day for seven days, notice how you are standing.

Now straighten up.

Throw your shoulders back. You can even do a few shoulder rolls to loosen things up.

Turn your hands so that your palms face the mirror, keep them wide open.

This is how a sovereign being stands. How do you feel?

You are meant to greet the world, not cower from it.

Smile.

Notice the vitality that your stance now emits.

You have so much love.

You are ready to share the surplus.

Meet your smiling eyes with expectation. Grin.

Have a powerfully loving day.

Welcome. Please follow along one day at a time.

This is not a race. Everyone wins on the Love Quest.

Day 1

Welcome to your Quest. In truth, although we talk about it for just one week at a time, it is ongoing. Life is the Ultimate Quest.

Personally, and globally you are being asked to declare what you know and who you are. There is only Truth. It rests in two words. *I am.*

Embracing truth is another thing altogether. Whether you are aware of it consciously or not, you are, with each decision, choosing. What this feels like depends on you. Contrast is everywhere. As One, we experience individual lives.

On these Quests we've explored love. Love is Truth. Love is Freedom. Love is us. What does that even mean?

Here's a personal story.

Most mornings you'll find me at a local school where my son studies jazz. There is a blind young man there each day; walking the neighborhood with an aide and a cane. I've watched him for six months now. At first the aide was right next to him with hands on and verbal instructions. Today, she's several paces behind not saying much. He is leading the way with a huge smile on his face. One day he'll walk on his own. Freedom.

In order to walk the Truth, we will need to give up our personal aide. What is your slavery/ownership crutch? Until you are willing to drop it, you are not free.

This is a process. Until recently, we didn't remember the truth of our being. We have a lifetime entrenched in laws and debt and ownership and rules and should and shouldn't. We are, right this very moment, defining what Love looks like as it walks around.

What do you have to let go of? *To feel the fullness of Agape you must stand unencumbered.*

It is a scary thing, to realize you walk alone here. Yet, this is a physical incarnation. The journey you are on now began with your first breath and will end with your last. No other being does that for you. It is you, all you, nothing but you. Who are you?

You are a spark of eternity, birthed from Source. You are equal in every way to kings and criminals, popes and prophets, beggars and beauty queens. Anything written or spoken that claims ownership or control over you is illusion. All are One. *There is no hierarchy of worth.*

As we begin this Quest, consider the "ties that bind". Whether they be rings, contracts, numbers, debt or laws does not matter – they signify ownership at some level. You are an eternal bit of

Love, unable to be bound. You have pretended, in a game of slavery, to be less. You are so much more than you know.

Realize that as you consider letting go of things, rings, rules and obligations – you are not changed. You will always honor the truth of your being. You cannot help but BE. No, you will not change, yet you will become the fullness of who you are; a fascinating, individual, indescribable and gorgeous bit of Love.

Like the caterpillar, you have built around yourself a cocoon, holding you in one place so that all of your focus could rest on what you came to do – transform. It is time to fly.

You are the One you've been waiting for.

See you tomorrow.

Day 2

You are on your journey, discovering what it is to love. It is not what you've been told. Words like sacrifice, selfless and obey have managed to crawl into the same sentence with love, honor and cherish. They are interlopers, planted there to infuse the field with doubt, debt, fear and worth. Love is a field of wildflowers. It self generates and spreads with random abandon, knowing no boundaries, borders or requirements. Love simply is. Love is what you are.

You came here to be part of a grand experiment. In it, you've been surrounded, since birth, with falsehoods and half-truths. They have told you there are things you must do, rules you must follow, ways you must look, amounts you must have, words you must say, groups you must be a part of and attitudes you must adopt in order to be worthy of anything desirable. Love, prosperity, expansion and joy were properties of the rich and elite; or so you were told. You were taught the concept of work, which in itself is neither good nor bad. Yet what you also learned was that work was necessary in order to "deserve" anything positive. All the while, you watched a small fraction of the population who seemed to follow none of these teachings – yet spent lifetimes enjoying both wealth and play. It was not a fair world – on purpose. This experiment has come to a screeching halt, the results are in.

The official report is yet to be released; yet preliminary findings tell an interesting story. Despite every effort and manipulation both on and off world to completely enslave the human, we have declared ourselves free. In each generation there have been the outliers, the misfits and the rebels — none of whom would succumb. Like the wildflowers, this field of humanity has continued to populate itself with relentless beauty and unstoppable passion. Humans Being have consistently, through every age, declared their sovereignty. A surprise to the controllers, yet not to us, is that despite all efforts to force us to do otherwise — we love.

For love is the force of creation. At the instant moment of our arrival, conception, there is passion unleashed and unable to be inhibited. Does it surprise you that the most exhilarating, satisfying and thrilling moments of your life were those in which you felt free? Passion is how you began — it is who you are.

Passion is the one thing that has been harvested and controlled. Religions, wars, laws and enslavement all work at controlling and manipulating your emotions systematically. That way they can be used as sustenance in a predictable fashion.

Yet you, a wondrous Human Being, have loved anyway with reckless abandon. You've loved when you wanted to, who you wanted to and how you wanted to. Now that the experiment is over you can love yourself the same way. Realize that conditions of worth are lies – you are unconditionally worthy of love. Without restriction – adore who you are.

Care for each part as you would a newborn. Gently caress, lovingly engage and joyfully embrace each facet that makes you – you. You are perfection.

There is nothing to give up in order to get agape. Agape is your birthright. Love is truth. You have come to shine your light on all those dark places we've been focused – to point the way to freedom. It is your brilliance that broke through every attempt at ownership. Remember who you are. You are the One we've been waiting for.

See you tomorrow.

Day 3

It is your third day and you are in it now. As you navigate the journey you notice obstacles. There are many ways to get there, all leading home. How will you know when you arrive?

I once heard Barry Neil Kaufman (The Option Institute, author of "Son Rise") describe what it was like to be in a love relationship that was both intimate and equal. He said (and I paraphrase) "Being with Samahria is like being alone. I never worry about what I am saying or not saying, doing or not doing. I just Am."

I've thought about that ever since, it seemed such an odd response. He didn't say "She completes me" or "She's the best thing that ever happened to me". He didn't put her in any place above or below himself. In fact, he seemed to be saying it didn't matter if she was in the room or not. Yet if you saw them together, you would recognize a deep and mutual love, coupled with intimacy.

This is absolute freedom. All have equal value here. This place has no owners. There are collaborators here. Partners. Co-creators. Teams of equals. Humans *Being*.

There are no Humans Owning. There are no Humans Owing. Debt is non-existent. In relationship to each other, we negotiate and agree or not; all the while respecting the worth of each other. We do not withhold for personal gain, to hold the advantage, the upper hand, or more. More of WHAT? All are ONE.

Wrap your head around ONE. What are you holding on to that separates? What false notions of slavery and ownership are you stuck on? What is blocking your personal path? What boulder are you looking at? Consider them now; you are on a Quest for Agape. Absolute Freedom. Unconditional Love. Love with exception or condition. Just love.

We all arrive unencumbered. To Love unconditionally is to simply BE. Wherever you are. The burden of ownership is invented. It has inhibited, contained and controlled you. It implies the false notion that you control the life force of another. This is never true. All are One. The force of Life that runs through everything springs from One Source.

This Force courses through all that you see. People, animals, plants, earth, water, minerals, sky – are alive and intelligent and absolute. We may play together, sharing time, space and responsibilities. Yet at no time in our game do we stop being free.

Even the best actors at some point take off their costuming, let down their hair and relax.

Deep in your Quest now, see ownership for what it really is; a burden. Ownership promises control and safety and power. Ownership is a lie. You can use each other, play with each other and always, always love each other. What you will never do is own each other. *If someone believes they are indebted to another person/corporation or owned by another person/corporation, they are enslaved by their own belief - they are not enslaved by the "other". There is no "other". There is only One.*

You are not powerful because of what or who you "have". You are powerful. You are not worth more or less because of a bank account or a marriage license or a title. You are worthy. Let go of illusory things that seem to be holding you together. Know that you are enough.

You stand without requirement. So, does everyone and everything else.

You are perfect. Period. End of story. Breathe. Feel the fullness of your Being. Love without explanation or the burden of control. Love with wild abandon. Love all of the players in this game. It is a grand, surprising and enthralling party. Let go and love every Being in attendance. We are all here on purpose – as One.

We are the One we've been waiting for.

See you tomorrow.

Day 4

Midpoint now, you are faced with a decision. You can stop here and go back to your game of pretend, or you can forge ahead with authority to embrace the truth. Agape is but a decision away.

What will it take for you to love absolutely? Radical honesty. What is stopping you is fear of loss. What is at stake now is illusory. In truth, you do not own/control the "other". You are playing together and they come to you freely. They stay by choice; theirs, not yours. This is true of people, money and material things. There is not fear without rules. There is an exhilarating sense of self. Love comes when it is allowed, not forced. Love emerges when control falls away.

If you proceed now, you'll do so with blinders and masks off. To those still playing the game, this may look reckless, weird, disturbing or even wrong. It's okay, they are looking at shadows, mirror images and costumes – not you. They still believe the game is real.

Do you? In this Quest you are searching for unconditional self-Love. Trust is necessary. Self-Acceptance. Allowing. Being. Transparency. Truth.

What stops you in your tracks? Do you realize who you are? You are the physical embodiment of love. You are meant to run free. The whole world awaits your expansion and expression. You are not meant to be contained. Contrary to everything you've been told, you will remain and steadfastly love without a ring, contract, law or official to hold you firmly in place.

Love is what you do. Free is what you are. Go ahead. Try it. Let go of something you've held onto because you've been afraid. Watch what happens without the props. You'll discover you were there all along. Perfect.

Capable, authentic, brilliant and bursting with talent — there you are. You were built from Love and are here to Love. You do not need anything but you.

It is you that you've been waiting for.

See you tomorrow.

Day 5

Today you begin the final stretch for this Quest. It is your range of vision that determines the proximity of the goal. How far are you looking ahead?

What is known about some humans is that as they age, they tend to trip and fall. It was assumed for a long time that this was due to physical deterioration. It turns out that this is not true. It is actually because of a change of focus. This change is the result of fear.

Some of us will start to limit our options and capabilities, while decreasing our world view and pulling back. As we walk, rather than focus on the where we are headed, we look at our feet. Fear sets in. We watch only each step we take. While we are doing so, we lose sight of the destination and miss all the scenery. Sometimes, we trip.

It is not our feet that decide our success or failure at walking; not only our feet anyway. It is our brain, our sense of balance that keeps us upright and moving always forward. We were meant to hold our head up and look the way our eyes are pointed – ahead. The more we take in about the surrounding landscape, the greater success we'll have navigating the terrain.

Look ahead, around and at everything. There is so much to see and a great deal to love. It is fear that holds your head down, cautious and unsure. Confidence, determination and pleasure will carry your gaze to the finish line, seeing the outcome you desire. What you see is what you'll get. If you only look down, you'll end up on the ground.

See yourself as you've ever wanted to be. Your imagination is your greatest tool. You are in a time of manifesting miracles. What lovely, happy version of yourself are you becoming?

This is not to make light of or ignore the very real people, things and institutions that can trip you up. This is a call for clarity of vision and lack of fear. It is not just your feet that will take you there. It is your head and even more so − your heart.

As you widen and expand your sight, you notice things you missed before − things to love, to tenderly care for, to laugh with, and to smile at; things that excite and thrill you. You notice life. Love is not limited. It is expressed in every part of you and all you see. Look as far as you possibly can.

The end of this Quest is visible now. It only takes awareness. Look up and look further. See the possibility for you. Say yes. It is not just about the mechanics of getting from here to there, it is about how you feel along the way.

Expect success and look beyond your original goal. You will always want more. Anything you can envision you can create. Children are not limited in their imaginations until we plunk them in systems of "education", where their thoughts are measured and judged. We have learned well, it is time to unlearn.

You can love everything about yourself. Every bit of you is okay. Hold your head high and keep looking for the next best thing. All the while, appreciate the treasure of the love within arm's reach. It is all your belief, your focus and your gaze that sets up your reality. You may trip, and that's okay. Sometimes we do that to remind ourselves of what's important. Enjoy each step while you pay attention to the journey; and look up.

You are the One you've been waiting for.

See you tomorrow.

Day 6

Notice the light. With your mask now off and your head held high, you will see it in places you haven't before. Then an amazing shift will happen. You will take note of where it isn't. These places will stick out "like sore thumbs". This may come as a surprise.

You may wonder "How come I never noticed?" It is not for lack of ability or even interest. The masks, blinders and focus have been intentionally institutionalized. You've been a slave to each and the effort to proceed with them firmly in place has been exhausting.

Aware now of alternatives, you are like a moth to the flame. Inexplicably drawn to the brightest glow, you gather and watch. No longer are you content or even capable of staying in the dark. You have seen the light. It emanates from people, from some ideas, programs, food and entertainment. The more you watch it occur, the sharper the contrast appears. It's real obvious when it is absent. Your wings just can't take you there; it's too dark. In your heart, you feel its absence.

A well-lit person, place, thing or situation just feels good. You can breathe. You know. More to the point – you are recognized. You are equal. The truth of you is seen here. You speak freely and listen attentively. You desire to participate and do so with joy. You feel exuberance. "This is good." "It feels like home."

The light that calls you now is your own heart. It has opened and burst through any controlling, uncomfortable binding that held it before. You can love. You can trust. You are love. Just BE.

It feels like play. It feels like fun. Anxiety shows up only because it is so new and unfamiliar. Think back to that first moment you realized you were riding a two-wheeler without anyone running alongside, holding you upright — you were scared for a second. You may even have lost your balance. Then, you took off — free. With my first taste of freedom on a two-wheeler, I opened my mouth and screamed with joy. Then a fly flew in. I spit him out and kept on screaming, pedaling faster and faster. Freedom is adrenalin.

You were meant to feel wonder-full. You were born to love and be loved in return. Your power is within and you don't need another to tell you how to use it or to judge its worth. You ARE the light. This is the reason you notice it now. Your core, your eternal Being, is love. Without reservation or limitation, just BE; be that which you are.

Recognize that feeling of constriction and fear that wells up in your gut when confronting a falsehood. Then, without judgment, move towards the light. Your gut will tell you when you are out of the dark. All are equal here. You came now to play this end game. You came now to demonstrate truth. You are the light. However concealed, it rests within. Trust what feels good. You will find it there.

It is the brightest, strongest, most powerful way showers that are attending this party. You were one of the first in line. You chose this time now. It is the ultimate in visual, sensual, emotional sensation and you wanted every minute of it — you knew you'd persevere and emerge brilliant — radiating your light for us all to be illuminated.

You know what love is. It is there, in that moment of connection. The specifics are endless yet the feeling is ONE — recognition, joy, passion, fulfillment, freedom, exhilaration, peace; all are words for Agape.

You are here to love yourself despite all objections. Naysayers quiet down in the presence of your light. You are everything they'd hoped to be. They too, are inexplicably drawn ever closer, watching.

When you notice them, open your arms and whisper *"Not just me, but we. The light is brighter now that you are here. We are the One we've been waiting for."*

See you tomorrow.

Day 7

You've realized the final moments of your journey. Whether or not you are aware of it, your Quest is one the entire world is on. We are moving out of slavery systems and slavery thought processes. We are stepping into truth. This is the next dimension and the Shift in Consciousness we've waited for.

For your power has prevailed and led you ever forward. You have succeeded without holding any weapons. In fact, you've often been at the receiving end of their fire. Yet, you are here now, Being.

The power in your Doing has created this Shift. Have you felt it? It happens mostly subtly; sometimes out loud. Love has fortified your heart; in the darkest moments it has held you. You have never forgotten your truth.

You are beholden to none and you hold none. Free will is the only rule. Responsibility is key. Each of us takes it on full for every action – call it blame or call it credit; it belongs to you alone.

Agape is the game now. Self-love. Not at the expense of another, for there can be no expense in love. Love is free. Yet it is played in concert with the "other". All this time, when you imagined you were hurting your lover or your parents or your brother – the one you were hurting was you. All this time you've blamed your wife or your father or your friend for not loving you enough – it was you not loving you enough.

Do you get it? Can you see it? This was a game we all played – blame, judgment, hatred, doubt – so that when the moment came we'd notice the contrast and Shift.

That moment has arrived and we can see now the truth. None of us are victims – we are players. It is time for the good part.

Accept yourself. Accept each other. Thank the "other" for their participation; convincing and well played. Hug yourself and know that you are okay. You can focus now on truth.

In absolute honesty this life is but a brief moment of your eternal Quest. You can choose now to write the part for its remainder. Who do you wish to BE? You are pure gold – 100% solid love. The energy of Source runs through you. How will you spend it? You do not need value added to be worthy or to move forward. You know who you are.

Feel the truth of your worth. It may bring you to your knees in wonder and gratitude; yet not shame or remorse or sorrow. All is done, forgiven and over. Today is a new Quest. You've reached Agape. You see what it means to love yourself.

With your head up and your shackles removed — look for the light. You will notice it now — its reach expands with each expression of truth.

Loving yourself means loving the world — we are One. Let that sink in and revel in this feast of Agape.

Your Eternal Heart

Prelude

This week is all you.

Strut up to your mirror and stand tall with your shoulders back.

Take your two hands and place them on either side of your face.

Hold them there gently. Send love through all of your parts.

Watch your eyes soften as this love overflows. Tears may squeeze out and that's okay.

Say "I get it now."

Say "It was always and all ways you."

Say "I love you."

Welcome. Please follow along one day at a time.

This is not a race. Everyone wins on the Love Quest.

Day 1

You've embarked on yet another Quest. So many places we've travelled together and still there is further to go. For you have not seen what you are searching for, and you are an associative learner. Repetition and familiarity is what will jog your memory and sharpen your vision.

There is nothing familiar about Absolute Freedom. Unconditional Love is sovereignty. "Thou shalt have no other Gods before me."

Realize what the words mean. Examine the Gods in your life. Who or what is preventing you from Love Absolute? To Love is a fearless act.

Freedom is something we like to hear tales about and fight for. Yet fight and freedom are oxymorons. You must not fight for that which you are. You must accept that which you are and Be.

For *we are One*. There is no other. Love is your very essence and to realize itself does not require a fight. Do your lips argue over which is right? How could you kiss without the upper? How could you kiss without the lower?

The Gods before you have demanded subservience. You may say, "I have only one God." Yet I tell you this, any person, idea, law, situation or belief that requires your compliance before you are accepted — is a "God before you."

You require nothing. Agape is the force that propels your Being. You have come to this life fully prepared to embrace your truth, all the time floating on a sea of falsehoods.

For Agape and Freedom are synonymous. You are not here to be inhibited or limited or diminished. You are here to realize and be the essence of Eternal Love.

In your everyday, since you are on a Quest, this demands a noticing. Step back from your interactions and examine your role in them. Are you, at any moment, giving up a bit of yourself?

For Love is Free. It makes no demands. It has no requirements. There is not another who can take it from you, all is given.

If you feel you are controlled, then you have given your power away. To reclaim it, merely stand. You carry the truth, and regardless of the shouting and the doubting, the truth will not be stopped.

You are Free. What would you do right now if you were unlimited? I tell you this — you are. So, the question then becomes, what are you waiting for? You are the One.

See you tomorrow.

Day 2

And what does it mean to Love? For Love is not what you've

been told. There are not amounts or kinds or degrees. *Love is*

what you are and love is what you do. Love is the great equalizer,

unifier and pacifier. You have been restricted in your expression

of it so much that you've fallen into judgment. A ridiculous thing.

Do you stand in judgment of a flower as it grows? Do you say –

this one should not grow so close to that one or those two should

not cross pollinate. No. Yet we do so of each other and it

trivializes our beautiful minds. A flower grows; *a human being*

loves.

The fuel that enlivens us is the very thing that we are. It is

Love. We Love. Equally and Absolutely. The judgments we've

placed on our Loving are not because Love exists only in some

places and in some relationships and in some amounts. If the

word "some" were true, then the words "none" and "more" would

also apply. They don't. Not for this discussion.

There is Love.

There is never "none". We don't Love one "more" than the

other. We Love. Let go of words of judgment or quantity.

You are Love. A flower is a flower. Despite its size, color or piece of real estate, it stands — always a flower.

Love has been confused with so many things — beauty, obedience, physical attraction, happiness, cooperation, ease, comfort. It is none of these. *Love is core recognition of Truth.*

When you allow yourself judgments, they turn inevitably within — to the place where you find your harshest critic. *It is yourself you are the most afraid to Love.*

What would happen if you Loved yourself without restraint? How would it look to be okay with every disobedient, irreverent, awkward, rude, unattractive, sad, out of shape, lazy, broke, weird or uncooperative part of yourself? What kind of world would it be if there was unconditional, unrestricted loving?

Watch the wildflowers. Stand in a room filled with little ones. Witness the beauty of unrestrained growth and feel the energy of uninhibited passion. This is your birthright.

You spring from Source and from you Source is made manifest on Earth.

All are watching. What are you waiting for? You are the One.

See you tomorrow.

Day 3

Please enjoy this story...

"I was recently told of an African tribe that does the most beautiful thing.

When someone does something hurtful and wrong, they take the person to the center of town, and the entire tribe comes and surrounds him. For two days they'll tell the man every good thing he has ever done.

The tribe believes that every human being comes into the world as GOOD, each of us desiring safety, love, peace, happiness.

But sometimes in the pursuit of those things people make mistakes. The community sees misdeeds as a cry for help.

They band together for the sake of their fellow man to hold him up, to reconnect him with his true Nature, to remind him who he really is, until he fully remembers the truth from which he'd temporarily been disconnected: "I AM GOOD"."

You too can surround yourself with love. There are no reasons to hold back; anything but love is a wrong turn. The path to Agape is clear and simple. You are always okay — the spark of Divinity is in your very heart. Feel the love that fuels your soul. This is the core of Oneness.

Love yourself in every circumstance. Love yourself without condition. There is only one way to reach the end of this Quest, and you are the only one who can get yourself there. That voice within has been waiting such a long time to be heard — listen. "You are love" it is whispering, "You are here to show the way."

See you tomorrow.

Day 4

Welcome to your 4th day. You are right between the beginning
and the end of this Quest. Consider unconditional self-love. Do
you have it? What is stopping you?

The words "but" and "if" and "when" and "almost" have no place in
a sentence with Agape. You either do or you don't. You can't be
a little bit pregnant. You can't have a little bit Agape.

It is the same with Freedom. You can't be partially Free. Either
someone else pulls your strings, or they don't.

You know now, the Truth. The "other" only shows up as a
reflection of your state of Being.

So, the questions come again — Are you Free? Do you Love
yourself? Look around, you are surrounded with your answer.

You are looking for an unrestricted life. Consider the birds.
When the spirit moves them, they fly. Watch a toddler. She
wears, plays, sings, skips and does whatever makes her feel
fabulous. She Loves her toes, her voice, her body, herself. The
bird flies Free.

There is Source. Between you and Source is merely a thought —
know yourself. I AM. Everything beyond that is experience and

the reason you are here. You are able to imagine yourself restricted or limited or unworthy. Yet these are not reflections of Truth. They are illusions. Those mirrors have been taken down.

The Truth is Eternal Essence – the place where Gods hold hands. It exists in exuberance, excitement, laughter, joy, passion, brilliance, Love. It is Agape. For the One you are loving without restraint has 7+ billion Eternal Hearts. They know who they Be. They are watching you remember.

What are you waiting for? You are the One.

See you tomorrow.

Day 5

Welcome to your 5th day. You probably don't want to hear methods or ideas or best routes to our destination. You probably just want to feel amazing. You are shooting for fantastic. Agape and Freedom promise spectacular.

Contemplating both, *here's what your day looks like:*

You leap out of a warm comfortable bed. Remember how you did that as a kid? You can't wait to see what comes next. You run into the kitchen and enjoy a hug and a meal of fresh food, both which you have plenty of. You then spend the day engaged in Doing.

Your "work" includes always your passion. You are unrestricted in where you can do this and how you can do this and who you can do this with. You are acknowledged for your unique brilliance and enjoy contributing. *Life is your stimulant.*

What is absent are rules, requirements, debt. There is nothing you "should" BE or DO. You are Free to choose.

Love is not something you're longing for – it is everywhere. You may or may not live with a "significant other" but it won't matter – *all are significant for you.*

You don't have to hold on to Love with an iron grip. You Trust. Love is. When you look into the eyes of humanity you see it there. This is what fills you.

Excess amounts of anything are no longer necessary to complete and thrill you. Living full out is your drug. Loving absolutely is your high.

This way of life is yours today, if chosen. No longer willing to commit to ownership and its resulting slavery systems, *you must commit to yourself.* Freedom is full time. Love is constant focus.

You'll have to yank yourself out of anything other than fantastic. Tell yourself the Truth until every corner of your Being believes it, singing "Yes."

You are a Being of Light – embodied. Source had a thought, an imagining, and you were shot forth. The thought went like this "What would it be like to experience the fullness of creation as (...fill in the blank with YOU)?"

You are not your body or your role or your relationship or your failure or your success. You are light, a bit of source, a kiss of love, a whisper of energy, experiencing life.

There are no parts of you unworthy. You are the stuff of Gods, Source in a human suit and beholden to none. Commit to this Truth. Look in the mirror and greet God. Look around and say hello to the sacred.

Walk gently and with a deep knowing of respect, feel the Earth and all of us whom she supports. Honor the task set forth when Source imagined you. Create Amazing. You are all that has ever been required. You are enough. You are Eternal Essence Embodied. Nothing could be more thrilling than that which you are in this very moment.

What are you waiting for? You are the One.

I love you, I appreciate you, thank you.

See you tomorrow.

Day 6

When my sons were very small, they believed themselves rich. Regardless of where we went, this belief was validated. They were surrounded in value, everything was a treasure, and all of it was theirs. Their shelves and pockets overflowed with it all – reminders of adventures. Rocks, feathers, bottle tops, leaves, shells, bits of rope and wire were valuable because they said so.

You are on a Quest. By definition, this means you are looking for something. It would follow then, that this is something you believe you don't have. Your Quest is for Agape – unconditional love of self. And what is love? It is acknowledging worth, seeing value, and holding in a sacred place. It is completely self-defined.

What if you decided right now, to believe yourself rich? What if you decided right now, to believe yourself worthy? I tell you, you are both.

Love and value are self-defined. My oldest sons believed themselves rich and worthy until they felt the world tell them otherwise. My youngest still refuse to accept the world's definition, and miracle gifts of abundance follow them everywhere.

What if we all did the same? Oh, I know we've been beaten down and it will take constant vigilance, yet what is there to lose?

You are building your reality right now. Declare and decide what's valuable. I AM Absolute Value. I AM Original. I AM Source. I AM Eternal Essence. I AM.

I tell you this, if you knew the power and magnificence that you were – there would be no Quest. The idea of looking for what was there all along would seem like a game of peek – a – boo. It's only interesting to the baby. She is unaware you've never left and is thrilled each time you show up.

Just because you don't have eyes yet to see, doesn't mean you aren't brilliant. Decide and declare right now where your Absolute Value rests. It is in your very Essence, your Eternal Essence. It is there that we connect, like the leaves on the tree. Individual and unique, they spring from One source. Absolute value resides in your Eternal Heart.

What you are waiting for is within that heart of yours; that ever expanding, relentlessly loving Eternal Heart. Freedom, Value, and Agape are but a decision away. Once you see the Value in each of the leaves, you understand the importance of the tree. Unity.

What are you waiting for?

You are the One. Precious and powerful, brilliant and tender, passionate and quirky, it's been you right along.

I love you.

See you tomorrow.

Day 7

Today marks the end of this Quest and as well, the end of all the "Join Me on a Love Quest" events. They began as a response to a question, and that question has been answered. The time for searching, waiting and questing is over. It is time now to DO.

Oneness answers every inquiry you have posed. You and I and the trees and our "enemies" are One. What I do to you, I do to myself. We cannot escape the consequences of our thoughts, words and actions. We, in every sense, are One. We know this now.

The core that unites us is our Eternal Heart. This is a place you've forgotten, where in unison, we love.

You are there still and you remember each night, while you dream. Soon, these and other memories will ignite for you these truths – *who you have ever been, all you are capable of doing, why you are here, where you are from and what was your plan.*

You have come to this moment now, fully equipped with the truth of your power, your beauty, your brilliance and our unity. I believe we have helped each other get here so that we could help others. This will be a ripple effect. We are One.

Trust and know that all answers are within. I cannot predict your future, yet I can see what's ahead. We've opened our minds and our hearts and there is no closing them now.

In the final analysis, none of us are 100 % sure what an "end of times" actually looks like. It's not available on any social media platform or publication. No one has seen it and shown up now to tell us. Oh, there are voices that describe possibilities. We each have our favorites, some we believe and like; others we aren't so sure about and most we read every day, regardless of opinion. We're looking for something that's not here; not yet.

In these end times we are getting in no uncertain terms the manifestation of our deepest held beliefs. We've lived through generation after generation of manipulation by those who see us as one mass of humanity, here to be controlled. We are waking up and finding our voice and our truth. This life is ours to control. The key to creation is within. We know this now, so it's no more "same old, same old". We don't know what to expect, this is new territory and it's driving us nuts. We don't trust the "powers that be" to give it to us straight; we aren't sure who to trust.

Trust yourself. Your body, your heart and your soul know exactly what they're doing. Each has been waiting for you to stop running the program of low self-esteem, self-doubt and self-hatred. All this love you've been *keeping from yourself* but projecting onto a God, human, animal or cause — is itching to reach you as well. You just didn't know.

It's okay. We've been slumbering together, a sort of pre-cursor to Oneness. These are the End Times of Mass Deception. We have entered the Beginning Times of Mass Uncovering — The Age of Enlightenment. We are opening our hearts; this has not ever been done on such a mass scale while embodied, not here on earth.

Agape is like nothing you've ever felt. It is freedom. It is pure, unrestricted and fearless. *There are no doubts in a heart that knows truth.* In the face of every confrontation, challenge, hardship or setback — nothing is lost. Agape yields a constant state of abundance.

This is the secret the manipulators have used to keep us in a state of subservience, lack and slavery. Self-hatred is not natural, yet we've each felt it. If you want to completely dominate someone, create fear in them. Then, they will act or not act accordingly; always as a reaction to fear. Self-determination will not be a part of their repertoire. It is instead a life of self-preservation and safety. This is the life we are ending; the "end of times".

We've been here so long that we are in the habit of looking to someone else to tell us the truth. This, so we'll then know how to react. *Life is an active endeavor, not a reactive event.* The times of believing we are controlled by others more powerful than us are over.

There is no one more powerful than you. These are the end times. You don't need anyone to tell you what comes next. That's the whole point. You only need to trust your inner voice, and then tell yourself the truth. *This is how you create the beginning.*

We are God consciousness, seeing ourselves as if for the very first time – enamored with the vision. These are not times to fear or to look for someone else to tell us about. These are the beginning times; our start as Agape sourced Masters.

We are beholden to none. We are One. The voice of truth, this inner rhythm of love we all hear inside, has now seen the light of day. It's okay to love yourself. You are perfect; an expression of joy without limits. Treat yourself tenderly, lovingly and lavishly. Then, when your eyes behold the rest of us, they will be all filled up and overflowing with Agape.

We will be encased in a field of unconditional love; the state of divinity.

So, be giddy with your own magnificence. Consciously live the fullness of your love. Believe in the knowing you come to yourself. Trust your truth.

The game of duality is ending now. You are embarking on a new journey. This one you will attend with full awareness and absolute knowledge. Secrets, lies and confusion are not welcome. Truth, transparency, agape and freedom are the hallmarks of this moment.

I feel you, I feel us. We are beyond ready to move to the new. Here, all of us are leaders, answer givers and truth tellers. This is why the Quest has come to completion. It is time to lead ourselves. You know what to do.

These are the beginning times. They are worthy of the Masters who created them; they are worthy of you.

You are the One.

You have anchored the light.

It is done.

It has been a privilege.

The End

www.ingramcontent.com/pod-product-compliance
Lightning Source LLC
Chambersburg PA
CBHW062045270326
41931CB00013B/2950